D1327878

SPECULAR REFLECTION

QC 425
.L3
1971

Monographs on Applied Optics
No. 2

SPECULAR
REFLECTION

E. P. LAVIN, M.Sc., D.I.C.

British Aircraft Corporation Ltd

RECEIVED

JAN

McDonald
Observatory

WITH A PREFACE BY

W. D. WRIGHT

Professor of Applied Optics
Imperial College of Science and Technology

American Elsevier Publishing Company, Inc.
New York

4854

© E. P. Lavin, 1971

Published in the United States by
American Elsevier Publishing Company, Inc.
52 Vanderbilt Avenue, New York, New York 10017

Library of Congress Catalog Card Number 76-170295

International Standard Book Number 0-444-19593-9

Printed in Great Britain

Preface

by

PROFESSOR W. D. WRIGHT

Applied Optics Section, Imperial College of Science and Technology

This monograph is a further publication in the series based on M.Sc. reports prepared by postgraduate optics students at Imperial College. When an M.Sc. student prepares his project report he may have some three months to collect the necessary information and write it up. I am always surprised at the breadth and the depth with which a particular topic can be studied in such a short period of time, but students are young and generally very keen. This was true of Mr Lavin, and although he has extended his M.Sc. material in preparing the present text, the monograph nevertheless gives an impressive indication of the theoretical sophistication and experimental coverage of the original report.

The reflection of light from a polished surface is probably the first optical phenomenon which a boy at school encounters in the physics laboratory. He is no doubt delighted when he confirms that the angle of incidence does indeed equal the angle of reflection, but it would come as a great revelation to him if he were able to appreciate the many ramifications of theory and experiment which can flow from that simple observation. It may even come as a revelation to some optical specialists to discover the varied aspects of specular reflection which Mr Lavin explores in this monograph. I see it, in fact, as essentially a voyage of exploration in which much useful information is recorded: for example, on the factors which govern reflection, on its wavelength dependence, on means to suppress it when it is a nuisance, as it so often is, on how to measure it, and many other topics. I believe Mr Lavin's text will be of interest to a considerable audience and will stimulate new thinking in reflection optics and allied fields.

Author's Preface

The philosophical curiosity of man often derives from the simplest observations. It is likely that reflection studies have proceeded from primeval man pondering the identity of the face staring back at him from beneath the surface of a pond. The first systematic study of optics, however, of which there is any definite knowledge is contained in the writings of Greek philosophers and mathematicians such as Empedocles (*c.* 490–430 B.C.) and Euclid (*c.* 300 B.C.). Indeed an empirically formulated law of reflection was well known to the Greeks.

Major advances in the understanding of the reflection phenomenon had to await the development of the wave theory of light. This theory, improved and extended, enabled Christian Huygens (1629–1695) to derive satisfactorily the laws of reflection and refraction.

The phenomenon of polarization on reflection was discovered by Etienne Louis Molus (1775–1812) about the beginning of the nineteenth century. However, at that time no theoretical explanation was possible for this effect, but the wave theory continued to be developed. Augustin Jean Fresnel (1788–1827) may be considered to have finally put the theory onto a secure foundation when he derived the most generally useful relations governing the intensity and polarization of light rays produced by reflection and refraction. The theoretical development of the subject was essentially complete with the work of James Clerk Maxwell (1831–1879) establishing the nature of light as an electromagnetic radiation. Using the relations bearing his name a complete and intellectually satisfying treatment of reflection phenomena is possible.

I incorporate elements of this treatment in Part 1 of this monograph, deriving the basic laws of reflection. As Part 1 progresses I consider briefly the possibility of reflection from other than smooth surfaces. Although only a limited treatment is given it will be seen that there is room for considerable development in the theory of reflection from rough surfaces. Studies of specular and near-specular reflection, however, are essentially practical and tend to concentrate on clarifying the definitions of measured quantities or applying the data for a specific purpose.

The measurement of specular reflectance, the prime parameter associated with specular reflection, is considered in some detail in Part 2. The general form of the measuring instrument is described and examples given of the manner in which various research workers have approached the problems of measuring reflectance. I chose the particular examples to provide useful illustrations of techniques for a variety of measuring conditions such as infra-red and ultra-violet illumination, vacuum and low-temperature environments. In choosing examples, of course, it is difficult to know when to stop. Specific methods of measurement and measurement environments are legion. Almost all are of some interest. I could for instance have included a description of the automatic instrument developed by Rennilson, Holt and Morris (1968). This was designed to be carried by unmanned lunar landing probes to make *in situ* photometric measurements of the lunar surface material. Although apparently unique, the technique and principles involved in this apparatus are adequately covered by the theory and examples presented in Parts 1 and 2 of this monograph. Indeed, I would hope that my choice of examples is sufficiently illustrative of basic principles to be relevant to most other situations.

In developing the theme of techniques inevitably the question of aims and applications of the resultant data arises. Apart from brief references in the context of each technique the main treatment of applications is in Chapter 9. Of prime importance are the determinations of the physical and optical properties of surfaces and these are considered in some detail.

I should like to acknowledge the advice and assistance given to me by Dr K. H. Ruddock of the Applied Optics Section, Imperial College, during the preparation of the thesis that formed the basis of this monograph. Material thanks are also due to the British Aircraft Corporation which supported me financially for the duration of my studies.

A cursory glance at the Bibliography will show my indebtedness to the journals *Applied Optics* and *Journal of the Optical Society of America*. I am most grateful for the ready permission given by the editors of these journals for me to publish the data and figures referred to in the text.

My thanks are due to the publishers and authors of *Principles of Optics*, which I wish I had written, for permission to employ the mathematical treatment therein for the derivation of essential formulae.

Figures 56–59 are reproduced with the kind permission of OCLI Optical Coatings Ltd., Dunfermline, Scotland. Table 2 was kindly compiled by my colleague at BAC, Bristol, Mr A. G. Crowther.

Finally I should like to express my thanks to Mr Neville Goodman and Mr David Tomlinson of Adam Hilger Ltd, for their considerable advice and assistance during the production of this monograph.

BRISTOL   E. P. LAVIN

May, 1971

Contents

PART 1

Theory of Reflectometry

1

Introduction

When a plane wave falls on the boundary between two homogeneous media of different optical properties it is split into two waves: a transmitted wave proceeds into the second medium and a reflected wave propagates back into the first medium. The existence of these two waves may be readily shown by the application of boundary conditions governing the continuity of electromagnetic wave electric and magnetic field components.

If the boundary is a smooth plane the incident wave is reflected in a single direction (specular reflection) and its characteristics may be readily described by the classical laws of reflection. These laws are perfectly general in that they may be used for both conducting and non-conducting media with only slight modification.

2

Reflection from a Plane Surface

A plane wave incident on the plane surface interface of two media of different optical properties constitutes the simplest reflection situation. As such, it is suitable for the derivation of fundamental reflection laws. In succeeding chapters the formulae expressing these laws will be applied to, or modified to apply to, surfaces of more complex form.

2.1. LAWS OF REFLECTION AND REFRACTION

In the following pages the notation and treatment will be, essentially, that used by Born and Wolf in their classic work on optics (1964).

A plane wave propagated in the direction specified by the unit vector s_i(i for incident) is completely determined when the time behaviour at one particular point in space is known. For, if $F(t)$ represents the time behaviour, at another point, whose position vector relative to the first point is r, it is given non-relativistically by $F(t - r.s/v)$. At the boundary between the two media, the time variation of the secondary fields will be the same as that of the incident primary field. Hence if s_r and s_t denote unit vectors in the direction of propagation of the reflected and transmitted wave, one has, on equating the arguments of the three wave functions at a point r, (x, y, z) on the boundary,

$$t - \frac{r.s_i}{v_1} = t - \frac{r.s_r}{v_1} = t - \frac{r.s_t}{v_2} \tag{2.1}$$

v_1 and v_2 being the velocities of propagation in the two media.

4

If the boundary is the plane $z = 0$ then (2.1) gives

$$\frac{xs_i(x) + ys_i(y)}{v_1} = \frac{xs_r(x) + ys_r(y)}{v_1} = \frac{xs_t(x) + ys_t(y)}{v_2} \qquad (2.2)$$

This equation must hold for all values of x and y on the boundary

$$\frac{s_i(x)}{v_1} = \frac{s_r(x)}{v_1} = \frac{s_t(x)}{v_2} \quad \text{and} \quad \frac{s_i(y)}{v_1} = \frac{s_r(y)}{v_1} = \frac{s_t(y)}{v_2} \qquad (2.3)$$

The plane specified by $\mathbf{s}_i$ and the normal to the boundary is called the plane of incidence. Relations (2.3) show that both $\mathbf{s}_t$ and $\mathbf{s}_r$ lie in this plane.

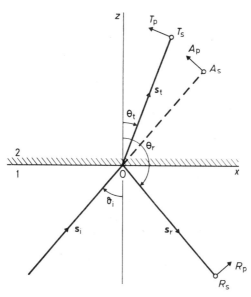

FIG. 1. Reflection and refraction of a plane wave. Plane of incidence.

Denoting the plane of incidence as the xz plane, with θ_i, θ_r and θ_t as the angles which $\mathbf{s}_i$, $\mathbf{s}_r$ and $\mathbf{s}_t$ make with Oz, then (from Fig. 1)

$$\left.\begin{aligned}
s_i(x) &= \sin\theta_i, & s_i(y) &= 0, & s_i(z) &= \cos\theta_i \\
s_r(x) &= \sin\theta_r, & s_r(y) &= 0, & s_r(z) &= \cos\theta_r \\
s_t(x) &= \sin\theta_t, & s_t(y) &= 0, & s_t(z) &= \cos\theta_t
\end{aligned}\right\} \qquad (2.4)$$

For waves propagated from the first into the second medium

the z components of the **s** vectors are positive; for those propagated in the opposite sense they are negative:

$$s_i(z) = \cos \theta_i \geq 0, \qquad s_r(z) = \cos \theta_r \leq 0,$$
$$s_t(z) = \cos \theta_t \geq 0 \qquad (2.5)$$

Using (2.4) with the first set in (2.3)

$$\frac{\sin \theta_i}{v_1} = \frac{\sin \theta_r}{v_1} = \frac{\sin \theta_t}{v_2} \qquad (2.6)$$

Hence $\sin \theta_r = \sin \theta_i$ and, using (2.5),

$$\cos \theta_r = -\cos \theta_i$$

Thus

$$\theta_r = \pi - \theta_i \qquad (2.7)$$

This relation together with the statement that the reflected wave normal $\mathbf{s}_r$ is in the plane of incidence, constitute the *law of reflection*.

Also from (2.6), and using Maxwell's relation $n = c/v = \sqrt{(\varepsilon \mu)}$ (n = refractive index, ε = dielectric constant, μ = magnetic permeability, c = velocity of light)

$$\frac{\sin \theta_i}{\sin \theta_t} = \frac{v_1}{v_2} = \sqrt{\left(\frac{\varepsilon_2 \mu_2}{\varepsilon_1 \mu_1}\right)} = \frac{n_2}{n_1} = n_{12} \qquad (2.8)$$

The relation $\sin \theta_i / \sin \theta_t = n_2/n_1$ together with the statement that the refracted wave normal $\mathbf{s}_t$ is in the plane of incidence constitute the *law of refraction* or *Snell's law*.

When $n_2 > n_1$ then $n_{12} > 1$ and the second medium is defined as being *optically denser* than the first medium. In this case, by (2.8),

$$\sin \theta_t = (\sin \theta_i)/n_{12} < \sin \theta_i \qquad (2.9)$$

so that there is a real angle θ_t of refraction for every angle of incidence. If, however, the second medium is optically less dense than the first medium (that is, if $n_{12} < 1$) then a real value for θ_t is only obtained for those incident angles θ_i for which $\sin \theta_i \leq n_{12}$. For larger values of the angle of incidence, so-called *total reflection* takes place.

2.2. REFLECTION FROM A DIELECTRIC MEDIUM

2.2.1. *Fresnel formulae*

Consider the amplitude of the reflected wave from the interface of two homogeneous and isotropic media of zero conductivity. These media are assumed to be transparent and their magnetic permeabilities to be effectively unity—that is, $\mu_1 = \mu_2 = 1$.

Let A be the amplitude of the electric vector of the incident field, with A complex. Its phase is equal to the constant part of the argument of the wave function; the variable part is

$$\tau_i = \omega \left(t - \frac{\mathbf{r} \cdot \mathbf{s}_i}{v_1} \right) = \omega \left(t - \frac{x \sin \theta_i + z \cos \theta_i}{v_1} \right) \quad (2.10)$$

Each vector may be resolved into components parallel (denoted by subscript p) and perpendicular (denoted by subscript s) to the plane of incidence. The choice of the positive directions for the parallel components is indicated in Fig. 1. The perpendicular components must be visualized at right-angles to the plane of the figure. The components of the electric vector of the incident field then are

$$\left. \begin{array}{l} E_i(x) = -A_p \cos \theta_i\, e^{-i\tau} \\ E_i(y) = A_s\, e^{-i\tau_i} \\ E_i(z) = A_p \sin \theta_i\, e^{-i\tau_i} \end{array} \right\} \quad (2.11)$$

The components of the magnetic vector are obtained by using the relations

$$\mathbf{E} = -(\mu/\varepsilon)^{\frac{1}{2}}\, \mathbf{s} \wedge \mathbf{H}$$
$$\mathbf{H} = (\varepsilon\mu)^{\frac{1}{2}}\, \mathbf{s} \wedge \mathbf{E} \qquad \text{with } \mu = 1$$

Thus

$$\mathbf{H} = \varepsilon^{\frac{1}{2}}\, \mathbf{s} \wedge \mathbf{E} \quad (2.12)$$

This gives

$$\left. \begin{array}{l} H_i(x) = -A_s \cos \theta_i \sqrt{\varepsilon_1}\, e^{-i\tau_i} \\ H_i(y) = -A_p \sqrt{\varepsilon_1}\, e^{-i\tau_i} \\ H_i(z) = A_s \sin \theta_i \sqrt{\varepsilon_1}\, e^{-i\tau_i} \end{array} \right\} \quad (2.13)$$

Similarly if R is the complex amplitude of the reflected wave, the corresponding components of the electric and magnetic vectors are:

$$
\left.\begin{array}{ll}
E_r(x) = -R_p\, e^{-i\tau_r} \cos\theta_r & H_r(x) = -R_s\sqrt{\varepsilon_1}\, e^{-i\tau_r} \cos\theta_r \\[4pt]
E_r(y) = R_s\, e^{-i\tau_r} & H_r(y) = -R_p\sqrt{\varepsilon_1}\, e^{-i\tau_r} \\[4pt]
E_r(z) = R_p\, e^{-i\tau_r} \sin\theta_r & H_r(z) = R_s\sqrt{\varepsilon_1}\, e^{-i\tau_r} \sin\theta_r
\end{array}\right\} \quad (2.14)
$$

with

$$
\tau_r = \omega\left(t - \frac{\mathbf{r}\cdot\mathbf{s}_r}{v_1}\right) = \omega\left(t - \frac{x\sin\theta_r + z\cos\theta_r}{v_1}\right) \quad (2.15)
$$

The transmission field vectors are found correspondingly.

The boundary conditions imposed by electromagnetic wave theory demand that across the boundary the tangential components of **E** and **H** must be continuous. Hence

$$
\left.\begin{array}{l}
E_i(x) + E_r(x) = E_t(x) \\[4pt]
E_i(y) + E_r(y) = E_t(y) \\[4pt]
H_i(x) + H_r(x) = H_t(x) \\[4pt]
H_i(y) + H_r(y) = H_t(y)
\end{array}\right\} \quad (2.16)
$$

the conditions for the normal components of **E** and **H** being automatically fulfilled. On substituting into (2.16) for all the components, and using the fact that

$$
\cos\theta_r = \cos(\pi - \theta_i) = -\cos\theta_i,
$$

we obtain

$$
\left.\begin{array}{l}
\cos\theta_i(A_p - R_p) = \cos\theta_t\, T_p \\[4pt]
A_s + R_s = T_s \\[4pt]
\sqrt{\varepsilon_1}\cos\theta_i(A_s - R_s) = \sqrt{\varepsilon_2}\cos\theta_t\, T_s \\[4pt]
\sqrt{\varepsilon_1}(A_p + R_p) = \sqrt{\varepsilon_2}\, T_p
\end{array}\right\} \quad (2.17)
$$

Note that equations (2.17) fall into two groups, one of which contains only the components parallel to the plane of incidence (p-polarization), whilst the other contains only those which are perpendicular to the plane of incidence (s-polarization). These two kinds of waves are therefore independent of one another. Equations (2.17) may be solved for the components of the reflected wave in terms of the incident wave components, again using Maxwell's relation $n = \sqrt{\varepsilon}$, giving

$$\left.\begin{aligned}
R_p &= \frac{n_2 \cos \theta_i - n_1 \cos \theta_t}{n_2 \cos \theta_i + n_1 \cos \theta_t} A_p \\[2ex]
R_s &= \frac{n_1 \cos \theta_i - n_2 \cos \theta_t}{n_1 \cos \theta_i + n_2 \cos \theta_t} A_s
\end{aligned}\right\} \tag{2.18}$$

These are called the Fresnel reflection formulae and were first derived by Fresnel in 1823.

They are usually written in the following alternative form, which may be obtained from (2.18) by using the law of refraction (2.8):

$$\left.\begin{aligned}
R_p &= \frac{\tan (\theta_i - \theta_t)}{\tan (\theta_i + \theta_t)} A_p \\[2ex]
R_s &= \frac{- \sin (\theta_i - \theta_t)}{\sin (\theta_i + \theta_t)} A_s
\end{aligned}\right\} \tag{2.18a}$$

Since θ_i and θ_t are real (the case of total reflection not being considered), the trigonometrical factors on the right-hand side of (2.18a) will also be real. Consequently the phase of each component of the reflected wave is either equal to the phase of the corresponding component of the incident wave or differs from it by π.

2.2.2. *Normal incidence*

In this case $\theta_i = 0$ and consequently $\theta_t = 0$. Thus (2.18) reduces to

$$\left.\begin{aligned}
R_p &= \frac{n-1}{n+1} A_p \\[2ex]
R_s &= -\frac{n-1}{n+1} A_s
\end{aligned}\right\} \tag{2.19}$$

where

$$n = n_2/n_1.$$

The distinction between p- and s-components disappears in this special case, the concept of a plane of incidence being inapplicable.

2.2.3. *Reflectance*

Consider how the energy of the incident field is divided by the two secondary fields.

The flow of energy associated with the propagation of an electromagnetic wave is represented both in magnitude and direction by the Poynting vector

$$\mathbf{S} = \mathbf{E} \wedge \mathbf{H} \tag{2.20}$$

using M.K.S. units.

From this the light intensity may be shown to be

$$\mathbf{S} = n\mathbf{E}^2 \tag{2.21}$$

The amount of energy in the primary wave, which is incident on a unit area of the boundary per second is therefore

$$J_i = \mathbf{S}_i \cos \theta_i = n_1 A^2 \cos \theta_i \tag{2.22}$$

and the energy of the reflected wave leaving a unit area of the boundary per second is given by a similar expression

$$J_r = \mathbf{S}_r \cos \theta_i = n_1 R^2 \cos \theta_i \tag{2.23}$$

The ratio

$$\mathscr{R} = J_r/J_i = R^2/A^2 \tag{2.24}$$

is called the *reflectance*. This quantity depends on the polarization of the incident wave and may be expressed in terms of the reflectances associated with the p- and s-polarization components.

If α_i is the angle which the $\mathbf{E}$ vector of the incident wave makes with the plane of incidence, then

$$\left.\begin{array}{l} A_p = A \cos \alpha_i \\ A_s = A \sin \alpha_i \end{array}\right\} \tag{2.25}$$

Let

$$\left.\begin{array}{l} J_{ip} = n_1 A_p^2 \cos \theta_i = J_i \cos^2 \alpha_i \\ J_{is} = n_1 A_s^2 \cos \theta_i = J_i \sin^2 \alpha_i \end{array}\right\} \tag{2.26}$$

and

$$J_{rp} = n_1 R_p^2 \cos \theta_i$$
$$J_{rs} = n_1 R_s^2 \cos \theta_i$$

Then

$$\mathcal{R} = \frac{J_r}{J_i} = \frac{J_{rp}+J_{rs}}{J_i} = \frac{J_{rp}}{J_{ip}} \cos^2 \alpha_i + \frac{J_{rs}}{J_{is}} \sin^2 \alpha_i$$

Hence

$$\mathcal{R} = \mathcal{R}_p \cos^2 \alpha_i + \mathcal{R}_s \sin^2 \alpha_i \qquad (2.27)$$

where

$$\left. \begin{array}{l} \mathcal{R}_p = \dfrac{J_{rp}}{J_{ip}} = \dfrac{R_p^2}{A_p^2} = \dfrac{\tan^2 (\theta_i-\theta_t)}{\tan^2 (\theta_i+\theta_t)} \\[3mm] \mathcal{R}_s = \dfrac{J_{rs}}{J_{is}} = \dfrac{R_s^2}{A_s^2} = \dfrac{\sin^2 (\theta_i-\theta_t)}{\sin^2 (\theta_i+\theta_t)} \end{array} \right\} \qquad (2.28)$$

Normal incidence. In this case again the distinction between the p and s components disappears and, from (2.19) and (2.24),

$$\mathcal{R} = \left(\frac{n-1}{n+1}\right)^2 \qquad (2.29)$$

It is seen from (2.29) that $\lim_{n \to 1} \mathcal{R} = 0$.

Similar values also hold for the limiting values of $\mathcal{R}_p$ and $\mathcal{R}_s$, as can be seen from (2.28), making use of the fact that, according to the law of refraction, $\theta_t \to \theta_i$ as $n \to 1$. Hence the smaller the difference in the optical densities of the two media, the less energy is carried away by the reflected ray.

2.2.4. *Polarization on reflection*

In Fig. 2 the reflectances for glass of refractive index 1·52 are plotted against the angle of incidence θ_i. The zero value of the curve (c), for $\mathcal{R}_p$, corresponds to the polarizing, or Brewster, angle, of arctan 1·52 = 56° 40'. The significance of this angle is seen by considering equation (2.28). The denominators are finite except when $\theta_i+\theta_t = \frac{1}{2}\pi$, since then $\tan(\theta_i+\theta_t) = \infty$ and $\mathcal{R}_p = 0$. For this case, see Fig. 1, the reflected and transmitted rays are perpendicular to each other and it follows from the law of refraction that $\tan \theta_i = n$. For light incident at the Brewster angle, Fig. 3, the electric vector of the reflected light has no component in the plane of incidence.

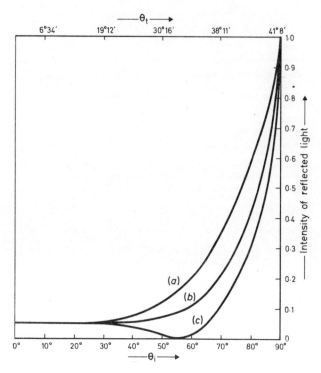

FIG. 2. Intensity of reflected light as a function of angle of incidence (after Chwolson, 1922). Curve a: $\mathscr{R}_s$, Curve b: $\frac{1}{2}(\mathscr{R}_p + \mathscr{R}_s)$, Curve c: $\mathscr{R}_p$.

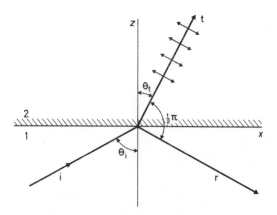

FIG. 3. Brewster angle.

Refractive indices with respect to air are usually of the order of 1·5 at optical wavelengths but at radio wavelengths they are much larger, there being a corresponding increase in the polarizing angle. For example, at optical wavelengths the refractive index of water is about 1·3 and the polarizing angle 53°. For radio wavelengths its value is about 9 and the polarizing angle is approximately 84°.

According to (2.27) the curve (*b*) in Fig. 2 is seen to correspond to $\alpha = 45°$. It may be shown that the same curve represents also the reflectance $\bar{\mathscr{R}}$ for unpolarized light, where

$$\bar{\mathscr{R}} = \tfrac{1}{2}(\mathscr{R}_p + \mathscr{R}_s) \tag{2.30}$$

With reflected light considered to be partially polarized, the *degree of polarization* is defined as

$$P \doteq \left| \frac{\mathscr{R}_p - \mathscr{R}_s}{\mathscr{R}_p + \mathscr{R}_s} \right| \tag{2.31}$$

This may now be expressed in the form

$$P = \tfrac{1}{2}\{|\mathscr{R}_p - \mathscr{R}_s|\}/\bar{\mathscr{R}} \tag{2.32}$$

The quantity in the brackets is sometimes called the *polarized proportion* of the light reflected.

The angle which was denoted by α, that is the angle between the plane of vibration and the plane of incidence, is called the *azimuth* of the vibration, and will be regarded as positive when the plane of vibration turns clockwise around the direction of propagation (Fig. 4). It may be assumed that the azimuthal angle is in the range $-\tfrac{1}{2}\pi$ to $\tfrac{1}{2}\pi$.

Then for the incident and reflected waves

$$\tan \alpha_i = A_s/A_p \quad \tan \alpha_r = R_s/R_p \tag{2.33}$$

Using the Fresnel formulae (2.18a),

$$\tan \alpha_r = -\frac{\cos (\theta_i - \theta_t)}{\cos (\theta_i + \theta_t)} \tan \alpha_i \tag{2.34}$$

Since

$$0 \leqq \theta_i \leqq \tfrac{1}{2}\pi$$
$$0 < \theta_t < \tfrac{1}{2}\pi$$

then

$$|\tan \alpha_r| \geqq |\tan \alpha_i| \tag{2.35}$$

In (2.35), the equality sign holds only for normal or tangential incidence ($\theta_i = \theta_t = 0$ or $\theta_i = \frac{1}{2}\pi$): the inequality implies that on reflection the plane of vibration is turned away from the plane of incidence. In Fig. 5 the behaviour of α_r is illustrated for $n = 1\cdot52$ and $\alpha_i = 45°$.

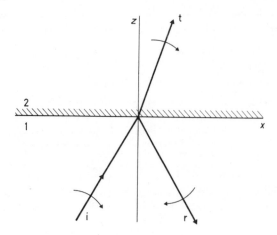

Fig. 4. Illustrating the signs of the azimuthal angles.

When θ_i is equal to the polarizing angle $56°\ 40'$, $\alpha_r = 90°$. In fact according to (2.36), $\tan \alpha_r = \infty$ (that is, $\alpha_r = \frac{1}{2}\pi$) for $\theta_i + \theta_t = \frac{1}{2}\pi$ whatever the value of α_i may be.

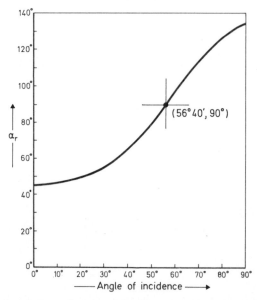

Fig. 5. Azimuthal angle as a function of angle of incidence (after Chwolson, 1922).

2.3. REFLECTION FROM A METAL SURFACE

It may be shown that the basic equations relating to the propagation of a plane time-harmonic wave in a conducting medium differ from those relating to propagation in a transparent dielectric only in that the real constants ε (dielectric constant) and κ (wavenumber) are replaced by complex quantities ε^* and κ^*. It follows that the formulae derived in previous sections, as far as they involve only linear relations between the components of the field vectors of plane monochromatic waves, also apply in the present case. In particular, the boundary conditions for the propagation of a wave across a surface of discontinuity, and hence the formulae of reflection and refraction, remain valid.

Consider the propagation of a plane wave from a dielectric into a conductor, both media being assumed to be of infinite extent, the surface of contact being the plane $z = 0$. By analogy with equation (2.8), the law of refraction is

$$\sin \theta_t = (\sin \theta_i)/n^* \qquad (2.36)$$

Since n^* is complex, so is θ_t and this quantity no longer has the simple significance of an angle of refraction.

Applying the concept of complex refractive index to the Fresnel formulae previously derived, expressions may be obtained for the amplitude, R, and the phase ϕ_R of the reflected ray by deriving expressions for the absolute reflection coefficient ρ and the phase change ϕ.

2.4. REFLECTION FROM A THIN FILM

If the second of the two media considered is given a small finite thickness rather than an infinite thickness the reflection characteristics change markedly. In fact the choice of material, and its thickness, deposited as a thin film on a semi-infinite substrate, enables reflection devices with desirable unique properties to be made.

As previously, the theory derived for dielectric materials may be used for conducting materials taking account of the change in character (real to complex) of certain of the variables involved.

2.4.1. *Dielectric films*

In previous sections the principles of continuity of **E** and **M** field components of the electromagnetic wave across a single boundary between two media were applied. A similar method is employed for the two, or more, interface thin-film problem.

At the *j*th interface (Fig. 6) the boundary conditions may be applied to give relations between the tangential fields in the two media, as before. If the $(j+1)$th interface was considered, similar relations would obviously be obtained. Thus the field equations

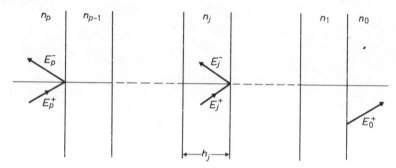

FIG. 6. Thin-film notation scheme.

at a discontinuity may be written as recurrence relations (taking the general, *j*th, interface) for application to a system of thin films—see Weinstein (1954),

$$E_{j+1}^+ + E_{j+1}^- = E_j^+ \, e^{ig_j} + E_j^- \, e^{-ig_j}$$
$$u_{j+1} \, (E_{j+1}^+ - E_{j+1}^-) = u_j \, (E_j^+ \, e^{ig_j} - E_j^- \, e^{-ig_j}) \qquad \Biggr\} \qquad (2.37)$$

where

E^+ refers to the tangential component of the incident field

E^- refers to the tangential component of the reflected field

$j = 0, 1, 2,..., p-1$

$g_j = \dfrac{2\pi}{\lambda} \, n_j h_j \, \cos\theta_j$ effective optical thickness

$u_j = \dfrac{n_j}{\cos\theta_j}$ (p-polarization) $\Biggr\}$

$u_j = n_j \cos\theta_j$ (s-polarization) $\Biggr]$ generalized refractive indices

In equations (2.37) it is understood that E_0^- and g_0 are identically zero. The equations are a set of $2p$ homogeneous linear simultaneous equations in the $2p+1$ unknown $E_j^\pm$; hence the solutions are

$$E_{j+1}^\pm = \frac{1}{2u_{j+1}} \{(u_{j+1} \pm u_j)\, e^{ig_j}\, E_j^+ + (u_{j+1} \mp u_j)\, e^{-ig_j}\, E_j^-\} \quad (2.38)$$

Equations (2.38) are a set of recurrence relations such that on assuming a given value for E_0^+, say unity, successive applications give $E_1^\pm, E_2^\pm, \ldots, E_p^\pm$.

Reflectance. In equation (2.21) the intensity of a beam was to be represented by

$$S = n\mathbf{E}^2$$

Thus if the total incident and reflected electric field vectors are $\mathbf{E}$ and $\mathbf{E}'$ respectively the reflectance is defined by

$$\mathscr{R} = \mathbf{E}'^2/\mathbf{E}^2 \quad (2.39)$$

Then, knowing the film constants, equations (2.38) may be used to derive the incidence surface tangential electric-field components. These, after simple allowance for the angles of incidence and reflection, may be substituted into (2.39) to give the reflectance of the thin-film device. Fig. 7 illustrates how this reflectance varies as a function of the effective optical thickness.

Phase change. The phase change on reflection is $\mathrm{Arg}(E_p^-/E_p^+)$ or, if E_p^-/E_p^+ is written $x+iy$ with x and y real, the phase change is $\arctan(y/x)$.

If, as is usually the case, the incident light is not plane polarized in or perpendicular to the plane of incidence the reflection factors for the two polarizations can be suitably combined. In the simplest case, if the incident light is plane polarized at an angle α to the plane of incidence it can be resolved into two fractions of which the amplitudes in the two directions are proportional to $\cos \alpha$ and $\sin \alpha$. The fractions are incoherent in the sense that they cannot interfere, although their phases are coherent, so that the effects in the two directions are to be combined incoherently.

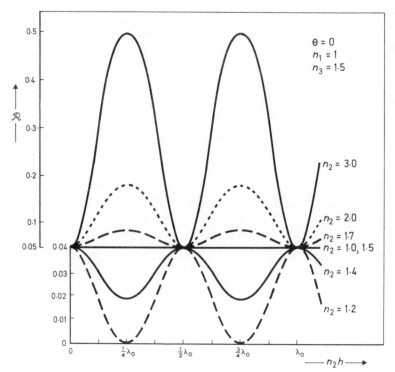

FIG. 7. Reflectance of a dielectric film as a function of its optical thickness (after Messner, 1943).

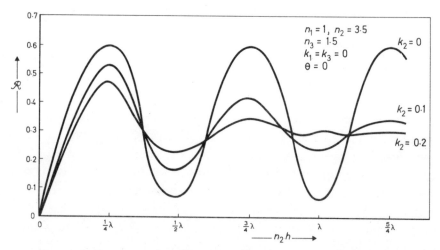

FIG. 8. Reflectance of a metallic film as a function of its optical thickness (after Hammer, 1943). k is the extinction coefficient.

2.4.2. *Metal films*

As mentioned in the Introduction (p. 3), the formulae for dielectric media as far as they involve only linear relations between the components of the field vectors of a time-harmonic wave retain their validity for conducting media. The proviso is again made that the real dielectric constant ε and the real wavenumber κ are replaced by their complex equivalents. It has been seen, in Fig. 7, that the reflectance for a dielectric is a periodic

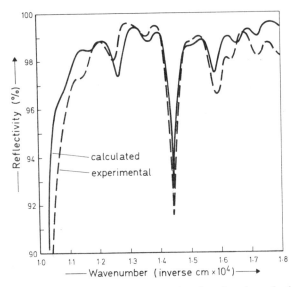

FIG. 9. Plot of reflectivity against wavenumber for the calculated and experimental wideband dielectric mirrors. The experimental curve is shifted to correct for an error in substrate position (after Berthold, 1969).

function of the film optical thickness with a period of half a wavelength. Now absorption is seen to reduce the amplitude of successive maxima and to give rise to a displacement of the maxima in the direction of smaller thickness (Fig. 8). At optical wavelengths, absorption of metals is so large that the thickness of material at which there is an appreciable transmission is well below a quarter wavelength. With transmitted light, therefore, maxima and minima are not observed.

It is obvious from Figs. 7 and 8 that by careful choice of the parameters comprising the optical thickness one can 'design' a thin-film device with predetermined reflection properties. This being said, however, it must be admitted that ensuring that the films conform to the required parameters is not an easy practical task. Berthold (1969) describes techniques for fabricating a wide-band dielectric mirror. These incorporate the use of a computerized prescription for the mirror which provides a means of

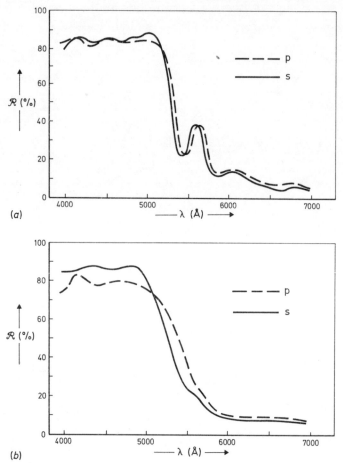

FIG. 10. Mirror spectral reflectance curves, p- and s-polarized light.

(a) Bandwidth	25–220 Å	(b) Bandwidth	105–870 Å
Range	4000–7000 Å	Range	4000–7000 Å

monitoring layer deposition. He obtains very good agreement between calculated and theoretical curves (Fig. 9).

Measurements made by the author of the reflectance spectra of two stellar interferometer mirrors are presented in Fig. 10. The mirrors, formed by a multilayer thin-film stack were designed to give better than 99 per cent reflectance at $22\frac{1}{2}°$ incidence, at a wavelength of 4358 Å. The instrument used for the measurements was the Wright spectrophotometer (see § 7.1.2) of the Applied Optics Section, Imperial College, London. Polarized light was used for the measurements, and the results for two effective bandwidths are given. The generally low values recorded must be attributed to various methods which were used to overcome detector sensitivity to imprecise location of the small, delicate mirrors.

3

Reflection from a Curved Surface

If a surface contains no structure of the order of magnitude of the wavelength of the incident radiation then this radiation will be specularly reflected according to the laws previously derived. This being said, however, the reflection characteristics of a body having such a surface will depend on the overall form of the body. Two forms which are amenable to mathematical treatment are considered and it will be seen that the method is essentially the application of Fresnel's formulae for oblique incidence.

3.1. SPHERE

Shoulejkin (1924) considered the problem of reflection from a dielectric sphere (Fig. 11). He derived the relation

$$I_r = I_i\, P \cos i$$

where

$$P = \frac{\sin^2 (i-r)}{2 \sin^2 (i+r)} \left\{ 1 + \frac{\cos^2 (i+r)}{\cos^2 (i-r)} \right\}^2$$

The proportion of s-polarized light in the reflected component has the intensity

$$I_{rpd} = I_i\, P' \cos i$$

where

$$P' = \frac{\sin^2 (i-r)}{2 \sin^2 (i+r)} \left\{ 1 - \frac{\cos^2 (i+r)}{\cos^2 (i-r)} \right\}^2$$

These results accommodate the concept of Brewster angle and this may be seen in the polar representation of Shoulejkin's results for reflection from a dielectric sphere (refractive index 1·32) in air (Fig. 12). He plotted the deviation angle γ where

$$\gamma = 2i$$

The value of γ at the Brewster angle of incidence is 105° 40′.

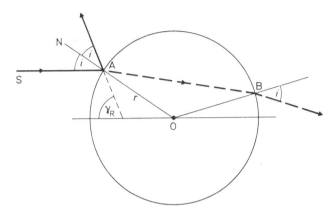

FIG. 11. Reflection and refraction at a spherical surface.

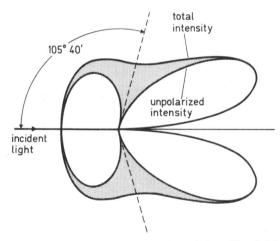

FIG. 12. Reflected intensity from a sphere (after Shoulejkin, 1924).

The question of specular reflection from a spherical surface was looked at in practical terms by Tousey (1957), who was concerned with the passive visibility of spherical earth satellites. He derived an expression for the luminous intensity, I, specularly reflected in a particular direction for an incident plane parallel (solar) beam of intensity E. His treatment was as follows.

Consider a cylindrical element, radius x thickness dx, of the incident beam. It contains flux

$$dF = E.2\pi x\ dx$$

This is incident on the sphere (radius R) between the angles i and $i + di$ and is reflected uniformly into the solid angle

$$d\Omega = 4\pi \sin 2i\ di$$

lying between the cones

$$\Omega = 2\pi(1 - \cos 2i) \quad \text{and} \quad \Omega + d\Omega.$$

The luminous intensity in the direction defined by Ω is

$$\frac{dF}{d\Omega} = \frac{E.2\pi x\ dx}{4\pi \sin 2i\ di}$$

For a sphere $x = R \sin i$, hence

$$I = dF/d\Omega = \tfrac{1}{4}ER^2$$

However, in this derivation Tousey makes the assumption that the point of observation is at a large distance from the sphere (that is, distance is much greater than R). It was later shown by Todd (1959) that the calculation could be generalized and that a similar expression could be derived for close observation of specularly reflecting spheres.

Again the sphere is illuminated by parallel light of strength E (Fig. 13). The cylindrical element of radius x and thickness dx contains an amount of flux

$$dF = E.2\pi x\ dx$$

which is incident upon the element of area dA_1 on the sphere, where

$$dA_1 = 2\pi R_1^2 \sin i\ di.$$

This flux is then reflected onto the element of area

$$dA_2 = 2\pi R_0^2 \sin \theta\ d\theta$$

of a larger concentric sphere. The illumination, I', at this surface on which lies the point of observation is

$$I' = \frac{dF}{dA_2} = \frac{Ex\ dx}{R_0^2 \sin \theta\ d\theta} = \frac{ER_1^2 \sin 2i\ di}{2R_0^2 \sin \theta\ d\theta} \qquad (3.1)$$

From Fig. 13 using the law of sines it can be seen that

$$\frac{R_1}{R_0} = \frac{\sin (2i - \theta)}{\sin i}$$

so that

$$\theta = 2i - \sin^{-1}\left(\frac{R_1}{R_0} \sin i\right) \tag{3.2}$$

and

$$\frac{d\theta}{di} = 2 - R_1 \cos i/R_0 \left\{1 - \left(\frac{R_1}{R_0} \sin i\right)^2\right\}^{\frac{1}{2}} \tag{3.3}$$

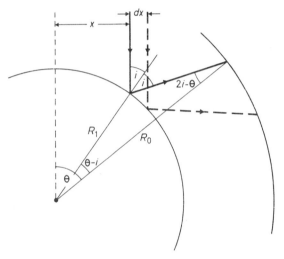

FIG. 13. Geometric construction for specular reflection from a sphere.

The expression of i as a function of θ in equation (3.1) would be desirable but cumbersome, whereas the results derived are such that the illumination may be readily computed for any values of θ and R_0/R_1.

Todd also points out that as the angle between the directions of observation and illumination decreases to zero equation (3.1) reduces to

$$I' = ER_1^2/(2R_0 - R_1)^2 \tag{3.4}$$

Since

$$\lim_{\theta \to 0} \left(\frac{\sin 2i}{\sin \theta}\right) = \frac{2R_0}{2R_0 - R_1}$$

As R_0 becomes much larger than R_1 equations (3.1) and (3.4) both reduce to

$$I'_{R_0 \gg R_1} R_1 = \tfrac{1}{4} E R_1^2 / R_0^2 \qquad (3.5)$$

This is Tousey's result divided by R_0^2 which follows from the fact that his result gives the luminous intensity or flux per unit solid angle whereas equation (3.5) gives the illumination of a surface normal to the direction of observation.

3.2. SINUSOIDAL WAVE

From the simple cases considered so far it is possible to extend theoretically the investigation to include much more complex shapes. Unfortunately in practice the mathematical difficulties increase rapidly and in the case of most real irregular surfaces either their contour is not known or, if it is, it cannot be represented by any mathematical relation. A special case, however, susceptible to mathematical treatment was described by Harrison (1945). He considered the equation

$$y = 0{\cdot}2679 \sin x$$

as representing a shallow sinusoidal wave, the maximum inclination of the side being $15°$. Fig. 14 shows such a wave illuminated by plane parallel light incident at $45°$ to the mean plane of the surface OX. Then the direction in which any particular ray will be reflected will depend on the slope of the wave at the point of incidence; and in fact all the light will be reflected between the limiting angles of $15°$ and $75°$ to the normal to the mean plane. The reflected light is thus scattered over a range of $60°$; but it is not uniformly scattered since the slope of the wave changes only slowly in the neighbourhood of $15°$, while at $0°$ it is changing much more rapidly. This may be seen by considering the slope θ of the wave profile which is given by

$$\tan \theta = 0{\cdot}2679 \cos x$$

In Fig. 14 the values of x for incremental differences of $1°$ in θ are shown. It can be seen that the spacing of these abscissae is not uniform; they are much more crowded together at the crest and trough of the wave than at the regions of greatest slope.

The ray incident at point A is reflected at $15°$ to the normal to the mean surface; the ray at B is reflected at $17°$ to this normal. All rays meeting the wave between A and B will be reflected at angles within the range $15-17°$; consequently the light flux reflected within this range will be proportional to the width of

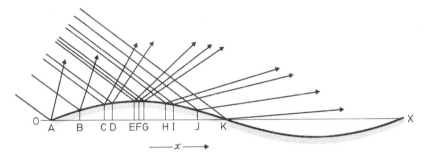

Fig. 14. Reflection of light by the wave $y = 0.2679 \sin x$.

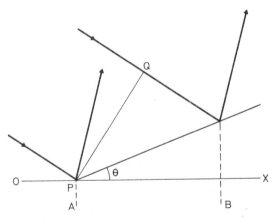

Fig. 15. The width of the incident beam.

the incident beam defined by A and B. This width (PQ, in Fig. 15) is easily shown to be $AB(1 + \tan\theta)/\sqrt{2}$. The width of the beam corresponding to CD is appreciably less because:

1. The distance from C to D is less and

2. θ is less.

Harrison gives tables showing the widths of the incident beams corresponding to $0.1°$ changes in θ, calculated by this method and expressed as a percentage of the whole beam covering a complete wave. He shows that the change of slope from 15·0° to 14·9° accounts for nearly 5 per cent of the width of the entire beam.

For the case where the reflection coefficient of the wave is independent of the angle of incidence, Harrison gives tables for the intensity of light scattered within an appropriate range of

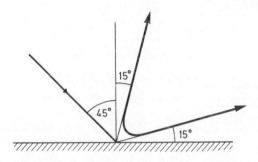

FIG. 16. Polar intensity distribution curve for 45° incidence.

angles. However, for the case where the wave is of water, Harrison incorporates the effect of variation of the reflection coefficient with angle of incidence. Considering Fig. 14, at A the angle of incidence is 30°; at K it is 60°. By Fresnel's law the reflection coefficient for water rises over this range of angles from

FIG. 17. Reflection of sky in ruffled water.

2·16 per cent to 5·92 per cent. Harrison thus gives a further table expressing his results as a percentage of the total light reflected by a complete wave, again for the same range of scattering angle. These results are illustrated in Fig. 16. No light is scattered, in this ideal situation, outside the range 15–75°; within this range light is indeed scattered but the intensity falls off very rapidly from the angles of 15° and 75°. Thus fairly well defined specular reflection is observed at two angles, neither of which corresponds to the angle of specular reflection for the mean plane of the sinusoidal wave.

Hulburt (1934) has shown that on account of the waves of the average ruffled sea, the light from the rim of the sea comes from the region of the sky 25–35° above the horizon and the reflecting facets of the sea which are visible to the observer are tilted up, on the average, about 15° from the horizon. The effect is shown in Fig. 17.

Time dependence. Longuet-Higgins (1960a), in his series of studies of specular reflection from random moving surfaces, also considered reflection from a ruffled sea. He found that light from a point source, the sun, produced a pattern of images, the image points corresponding to the maxima, minima and saddle points of a certain function. He was able to show that the images were generally created in pairs, a maximum with a saddle point, or a minimum with a saddle point and that the total numbers of maxima, minima and saddle points satisfy the relation

$$N_{mx} + N_{mn} = N_{sa} + 1$$

The process of creation or annihilation of images was studied in detail and it was found that over a period of time certain image points described closed tracks. Further work by Longuet-Higgins (1960b) consisted of ascribing Gaussian form to the moving surface and calculating theoretically the number of specular point reflections and the frequency of 'twinkling' as the surface moved.

4

Reflection from a Rough Surface

A number of theories have been developed to explain the scattering characteristics of rough surfaces. Unfortunately none of these theories is general and rigorous at the same time. In order to arrive at results that lend themselves to reasonably convenient numerical calculation certain simplifying assumptions must be introduced. Most important of these is the definition of a model of surface profile. Surfaces will, therefore, be considered within the general categories of those with defined profiles and those with random profiles. Defined profiles are more easily treated but random profiles are encountered much more often in practical applications.

By far the largest number of modern rough-surface scatter theories are based on the Kirchhoff approximation of the boundary conditions which are required to evaluate the Helmholtz integral. Beckmann and Spizzichino (1963, p. 59) derive the general Kirchhoff solution for the field scattered by a perfectly conducting periodic surface and apply it to specific profiles.

4.1. SINUSOIDAL PROFILE

The surface is represented by

$$f(x) = h \cos(Kx)$$

where $K = 2\pi/\Lambda$ is the phase constant of the surface and Λ is its wavelength. Using these relations in the expression for the general Kirchhoff solution, a relation is found for the reflectance as a function of the angle of incidence and the angles of observation.

This may be expressed in terms of a scattering coefficient ρ, which is defined as the ratio between the field reflected in a particular direction and the field reflected in the direction of specular reflec-

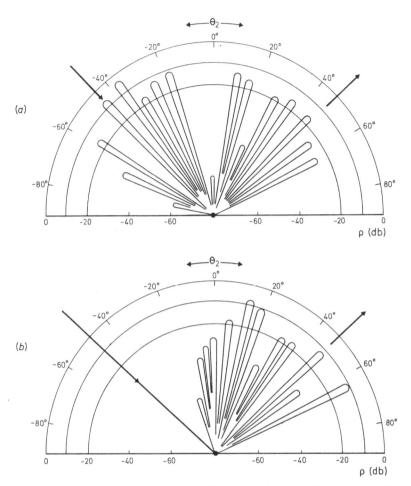

FIG. 18. Scattering by a sinusoidal surface (after Beckmann and Spizzichino, 1963).

$$(a) \quad \wedge = 10\lambda \quad \theta_1 = 45° \quad \kappa h = 10$$
$$(b) \quad \wedge = 10\lambda \quad \theta_1 = 45° \quad \kappa h = 3$$

tion by a smooth perfectly conducting plane of the same dimensions, under the same angle of incidence, at the same distance. Two scattering diagrams are given in Fig. 18 for a constant ratio $\wedge/\lambda = 10$, angle of incidence 45° and two values of κh, where $\kappa = 2\pi/\lambda$. As may be seen from these figures, diffuse scattering takes place for the relatively slight roughness $\kappa h = 10$ $(h/\lambda = 1 \cdot 6)$; and even for $\kappa h = 3$ $(h/\lambda = 0 \cdot 48)$, the maximum lobe does not lie in the direction of specular reflection.

4.2. SAWTOOTH PROFILE

A profile of this type (Fig. 19) contains two edges in each period and this militates against the use of the Kirchhoff method. However, Zipin (1966) describes the use of similar methods to

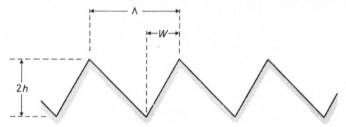

FIG. 19. Quantities defining a sawtooth surface.

investigate the effect on reflectance of mean slope and peak-to-valley heights of V-groove contours. He describes his results as 'satisfactory' inasmuch as measurements verify his two theoretical models.

4.3. RECTANGULAR PROFILE

Surfaces consisting of rectangular corrugations (Fig. 20) are met in waveguide theory and are therefore of some practical significance. For scattering in free-space propagation, the Kirchhoff solution will be inexact as there are now four edges in each period. An exact theory for this profile has been developed by Deryugin

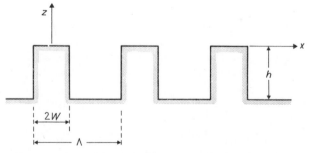

FIG. 20. Quantities defining rectangular corrugations.

and Myakishev, and Beckmann summarizes the principle and results of this theory in his book (1963, chapter 5). Deryugin's results are illustrated in Figs. 21(*a*) and 21(*b*) for lateral

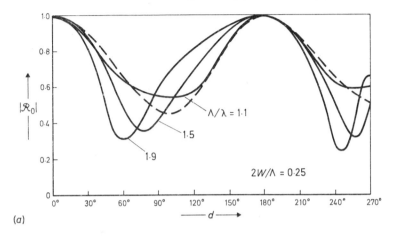

(*a*)

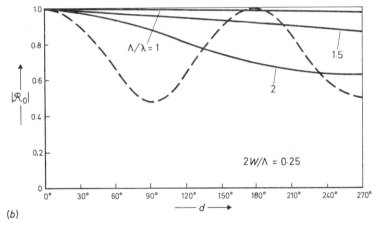

(*b*)

FIG. 21. Scattering by rectangular corrugations. Reflection coefficient of the specular mode as a function of the electrical depth, $d = (360\, h/\lambda)^\circ$ (after Beckman and Spizzichino, 1963).

(*a*) Lateral polarization—normal incidence.
(*b*) Longitudinal polarization—normal incidence.

and longitudinal polarization. The broken curves show the results obtained by a Kirchhoff-style method. Since Deryugin's method is exact it provides a clue to the validity of the Kirchhoff method. Considering that there are four edges to a period (and that the condition $\wedge \gg \lambda$ is not satisfied) one would have expected the Kirchhoff method to break down completely. In fact the discrepancy, especially for lateral polarization, is surprisingly small. Thus where no other method is available the Kirchhoff method offers reasonable generality.

4.4. RANDOM PROFILE

Surfaces encountered in practice are usually neither periodic nor explicitly given. Attempts have been made to develop rigorous theories for random surfaces and in doing so they classify the surfaces into two main groups; those formed by a random planar array of objects and those generated by a stochastic, or random, process. Having defined the surface, even if only as a statistical distribution and correlation function, it is possible to calculate the statistical distribution of the scattered field (see Beckmann and Spizzichino, 1963, chapter 5).

Chinmayanandam (1919) derived an expression having assumed that the reflecting elements of an optically rough surface have a distribution of Gaussian form. Thus

$$I(\theta) = \exp\left(-8\pi^2 \cos^2 \theta / a\lambda^2\right)$$

where θ is the angle of viewing

a is a constant.

For angles of incidence up to 54° this relation gives results in fair agreement with experiment. At greater angles Chinmayanandam cites the shadow effect of adjacent facets as the cause of failure. In this case he falls back on a complicated empirical relation.

On a far simpler level, J. H. Lambert, in 1760, postulated the quasi-empirical law which bears his name. He considered that for a perfect matt surface the intensity of light emitted in any direction must be proportional to the intensity of the incident beam, the cosine of the angle of incidence and the cosine of the angle of viewing. If, in Fig. 22, XY represents a diffusely reflecting surface illuminated by a beam IO, then the illumination at P will be

$$(cI_0/d^2) \cos i \cos \theta$$

where c is a constant defining the brightness of the surface, I_0 is the intensity of the incident beam and d is the distance PO. It follows that if I_N is the intensity of the radiation emitted normally to the surface then the intensity emitted at any other angle, θ, to the surface will be

$$I(\theta) = I_N \cos \theta$$

The simplicity of this law is deceptive; although quite a number of surfaces obey it approximately under certain conditions of illumination and viewing, no material is known for which it holds exactly. Thus H. R. Wright (1900) carried out experiments on a number of compressed powders (FeO, $MgCO_3$, and others) and found that for a fixed angle of viewing and varying angle of illumination the intensity of the light emitted is not proportional

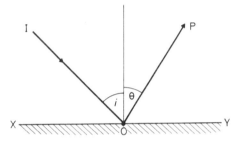

FIG. 22. Illumination geometry of a diffusely reflecting surface.

to $\cos i$, as Lambert's law states. On the other hand, with fixed angle of illumination and variable angle of viewing he found that the intensity of the light emitted was proportional to $\cos \theta$. He concluded that the law is strictly true for absolutely matt surfaces with a constant angle of illumination; the deviations otherwise observed are due to the $\cos i$ factor which introduces errors of from 4·6 per cent to 10 per cent. Wright did not examine materials with a marked structure and his results are therefore independent of the azimuth of the planes of illumination and viewing.

Unlike specularly reflecting surfaces, the perfect matt surface does not polarize the light falling upon it at any angle; if the incident light is polarized, the scattered light is depolarized (see Beckmann and Spizzichino, 1963, chapter 8). This, however, holds good only for near-white materials; as the absorption increases the light reflected from the specimens becomes more and more strongly polarized, whether the incident light is polarized or not.

PART 2

Practical Reflectometry

5

Introduction

In Part 1 of this study certain relations describing the phenomenon of specular reflection were established. These relations were capable of rigorous derivation due to the well defined nature of the geometrical problem. When rough surfaces were considered it was seen that no general theory could be developed to describe the mixture of specular reflection and diffuse scattering which is observed. However, some relations were derived for surfaces with mathematically specifiable profiles.

The practical measurement of reflectance requires considerable further qualification of the basic theoretical treatment already given. Consideration must be given to precise definition of the quantities being measured, the measuring instrument and the correct interpretation of the resulting data. Into this last category falls the use of reflectance data for determining the optical constants of reflecting materials. All of the reflectance relations derived in Part 1 were either explicit or implicit functions of parameters describing the electromagnetic properties of the interface media. Reflectance data, rigorously derived and interpreted, is thus a convenient and effective means of investigating these properties.

6

Practical Definitions

If radiant energy is incident on an element of surface at an energy flow rate F_i and is reflected by the element of surface at a rate F_r the ratio F_r/F_i is called the reflectance of the surface (this is merely a first expansion of the definition given in § 2.2). Furthermore, if the detector of radiant flux employed has, like the human eye, a spectral sensitivity that is wavelength dependent, the ratio of fluxes so evaluated is still called reflectance with a qualifying adjective (such as luminous, if the detector evaluates the flux in accord with the standard luminous-efficiency function). If, however, attention is confined to incident energy of fixed wavelength composition, or to detectors the spectral sensitivities of which are strictly independent of wavelength, it is still necessary to define one's terminology precisely. The problem arises because of the various angular conditions of incidence and collection used in reflectometry, and because most reflectometers do not measure the ratio of fluxes directly but employ specular (or diffusing) surfaces of known reflection characteristics as standards.

Thus, the quantities involved in the measurement of reflectance must be qualified by appropriate adjectives. Considering the collected flux, the adjectives are hemispherical, conical, or directional referring to all of the collected flux, to the part within a finite solid angle less than 2π steradians, or confined to essentially one direction (Fig. 23). To specify completely the type of reflectance measurement, the qualifying adjective specifying angles of collection may itself be preceded by similar adjectives.

6.1. JUDD'S NOTATION

Judd (1967) has proposed a notation to specify reflectance types. He defines the reflectance $\mathcal{R}$ as the ratio of some specified portion of the reflected flux to incident flux. The symbol $\mathcal{R}$ is followed by a two-part notation in parenthesis, the two parts being separated by a colon; the first part identifies the angles of incidence; the second, those of collection. Hemispherical incidence is notated 2π for the solid angle subtended by the hemisphere. Conical incidence is notated g for the geometry of incidence. If the cone to be specified is a right circular cone, g may be written: a_0, t_0, f_0, where a_0 is the half-angle of the cone, t_0 and f_0 are angles specifying the direction of its axis; thus t_0 is

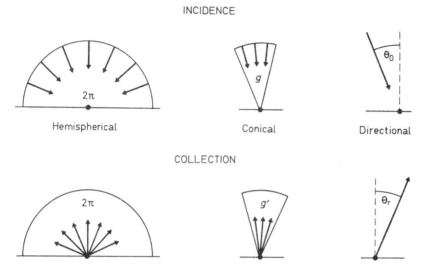

INCIDENCE

Hemispherical   Conical   Directional

COLLECTION

FIG. 23. The conditions of incidence and collection (after Judd, 1967).

the angle that the axis of the cone makes with the normal to the element of surface and may be called zenith angle or polar angle; f_0 is the azimuth angle or longitude.

Most actual reflectometers irradiate the specimen along angles bounded by a right circular cone. If a reflectometer has more complicated angular conditions of incidence the symbol g must stand for these conditions, however complicated they may be (for these complicated cases, as well as for the simple cases, g must be explicitly defined). Directional incidence is notated simply by the zenith angle t_0 and the azimuth f_0 of this direction.

Judd lists the nine possible reflectances using this notation and derives relationships between them by determining their values for the perfect mirror and the perfect diffuser — two extreme conditions.

6.2. PERFECT MIRRORS

Judd defines the perfect mirror as a surface such that, when irradiated within an elemental solid angle centering on the direction t_0, f_0 from specimen to source it reflects all of the incident energy within an elemental solid angle $d\omega = \sin t_0 \, dt_0 \, df_0$, centered on the direction t_r, f_r where $t_r = t_0$ and $f_r = f_0 + \pi$. For these viewing angles, the bi-directional reflectance of a perfect mirror is unity; but for any other angles, zero.

The directional-conical reflectance of a perfect mirror is unity if the direction t_0, f_0 coincides with any part of the mirror image g of g; otherwise it is zero. The conical-directional reflectance is similarly zero if the direction t_r, f_r fails to coincide with any part of the mirror image of g; otherwise it is

$$\cos t_r \, d\omega' / \int_\omega \cos t_0 \, d\omega$$

which approaches zero. The biconical reflectance of the perfect mirror is the integral of $\cos t_r \, d\omega'$ for the range of overlap between g and the mirror image of g', divided by the integral of $\cos t_0 \, d\omega$ over the solid angle ω specified by g.

6.3. ANGULAR CONDITIONS USED FOR MEASUREMENT

If the reflectance of the perfect mirror is unity for a given set of angular conditions, the ratio of the flux reflected by any specimen to that reflected by the perfect mirror will be numerically identical to the reflectance itself of the specimen. The perfect mirror, thus, may serve as a reflectance standard with a value of unity for these kinds of reflectance, and actual mirrors may serve as standards with appropriate values less than unity. All kinds of hemispherical collection conditions are eligible for this as are also some choices of angles for directional incidence. The other four kinds of angular conditions require evaluation of the reflectance of the specular surface used as standard for the particular condition: hemispherical-conical, hemispherical-directional, bi-conical, and conical-directional conditions; on this account mirrors are inconvenient for these kinds of reflectance. Only those conditions for which the mirror surface has zero reflectance (some choices of conical-directional, directional-conical, and bi-directional), however, are actually ineligible.

In applying these concepts to the measurement of specular reflectance, angular conditions involving hemispherical incidence or collection are of no value since they do not permit the identification of definable specular components. Thus there are four kinds of angular conditions on which instruments to measure specular reflectance could be based:

Bi-directional
Bi-conical
Conical-directional
Directional-conical

In practical terms the adjective 'directional' would be applied to a plane parallel beam reflected into a detector of small angular subtense at the surface. The term conical would not be permitted to cover all angles of incidence and collection less than 2π. Instead, in the context of specular reflection measurements, it must be viewed as a slight, definable, extension of the directional condition.

7

Measuring Instruments

It is perhaps a misnomer to refer to the apparatus for measuring specular reflection as *an* instrument. In fact the apparatus is composed of several elements, which may be variously disposed for particular tasks, and there are only a few commercial instruments combining them all. Thus it is reasonable to consider these elements separately under the headings of source, specimen, and detector.

7.1. SOURCE

The type of source chosen for a particular apparatus will depend very much on the foreseeable applications of the apparatus. The illuminating engineer, requiring data on reflectances of pavement surfaces (sunlight/sodium light), ceiling materials (neon/mercury) and so on, will specify the required illumination. The physicist's requirement for a mirror of 95 per cent reflectance peak at $0.4582\,\mu$ (bandwidth $0.0600\,\mu$), with some specified reflectance requirement over the rest of the visible spectrum, indicates that measurements need to be made over a wide spectral range. The first type of situation, where the source is merely a lamp complying to specific requirements of use, will not be considered in detail here.

The 'variable wavelength' source required for the investigation of spectral dependence of reflectance is called a monochromator and consists essentially of a white light source, a dispersing element (prism or grating), and a means of isolating selected wavelengths from the spectrum produced. When a detector is added to the monochromator, the instrument becomes a spectrophotometer.

Since, in measurement, the accuracy of the wavelength determination is dependent on the monochromaticity of the beam it is necessary to consider how this quantity is affected by various factors inherent in the design of the instrument. A discussion of these factors will make reference to the diagram of a simple spectrophotometer in Fig. 24. (The dispersing element shown is a prism but practically there is little to choose between the prism and the diffraction grating (Crawford and Marsh, 1957);

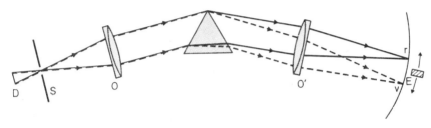

Fɪɢ. 24. Principle of the spectrophotometer.

S Slit.   o,o′ Collimating lens.
D Diffuse source.   r Red limit.
E Image of slit.   v Violet limit.

the prism gives a single spectrum and a low proportion of scattered light whilst the diffraction grating offers the advantages of angular dispersion being a linear function of wavelength, for small angles, and greater latitude in the physical size of the dispersing element.)

7.1.1. *Slit width*

The slit S is the effective source of the monochromator, light passing through it from the diffuse source D to fill the aperture of the collimator completely. The optical system images the slit at E; however, the prism disperses the incident light into its constituent wavelengths, each one of which forms its own image of the slit. Thus for a white light source a continuous spectrum is produced consisting of overlapping images of the entrance slit.

Reduction of the breadth of S produces two results:

1. The breadth of each image, and therefore, in the case of a continuous spectrum, the luminance of the band of light, is everywhere reduced in the same ratio as the slit width.

2. The reduction of the image breadth decreases the range of
wavelength present at any given point in the spectrum, so
that the 'purity' of the spectrum is increased.

If the distance between the centres of the images corresponding
to wavelengths λ and $\lambda + d\lambda$ is dx, and if the image breadth at this
wavelength is b, it follows that at any given point in the spectrum
one edge of the image formed in light of wavelength λ will
coincide with the other edge of the image formed in light of
wavelength $(\lambda + b \, d\lambda/dx)$. Hence at any point of the spectrum the
luminance is due, not to light of wavelength λ alone but to light
of all wavelengths lying between λ and $(\lambda + b \, d\lambda/dx)$ and this
range is directly proportional to b (and therefore to the slit
width) and to $d\lambda/dx$. Because of diffraction, there is a theoretical
limit to the degree of purity that can be obtained in the continuous
spectrum of a monochromator. Although this limit can only
be reached by the use of an infinitely narrow slit, yet a purity of
6 per cent less than the maximum can be obtained with a slit
width equal to $f\lambda/2D$ where f and D are the focal length and
diameter, respectively, of the collimator (Schuster, 1905). For
most monochromators f/D is about 16. The use of such a narrow
slit as that indicated by this formula is generally impossible,
except when dealing with the middle part of the spectrum of a
very bright source.

It is possible to apply a correction for the error due to finite slit
width. A simplified version of the rather lengthy original
treatment of this problem has been given by Walsh (1958,
p. 367).

Let the intensity curve of the impure spectrum of the standard
source as seen in the focal plane be represented by $F(\lambda)$, and let
the ratio of the intensities at any wavelength λ be $p(\lambda)$. In Fig. 25
let the curve ABC represent the function $p(\lambda)F(\lambda)$ and let OP
represent a given wavelength λ. Let PM and PN each represent a
wavelength interval equal to $\frac{1}{2}(a+b)$, where $2a$ and $2b$ are,
respectively, the breadths of the collimator and telescope slits
in terms of the wavelength scale of the monochromator. Let
BD $= \delta(\lambda)$. Then it may be shown that if $n \equiv b/a$

$$\frac{\phi(\lambda)}{f(\lambda)} = \frac{(p(\lambda)F(\lambda) - l \, \delta(\lambda) + m \, \delta'(\lambda) - \ldots)}{(F(\lambda) - l \, \delta_0(\lambda) + m \, \delta_0'(\lambda) - \ldots)}$$

where

$$l = (1+n^2)/6(1+n)^2$$

$$m = (6+5n+10n^2+5n^3+6n^4)/180(1+n)^4$$

$\phi(\lambda)$ and $f(\lambda)$ are the energy distribution curves of the test source and standard source, respectively.

$\delta_0(\lambda)$ is found in the same manner as $\delta(\lambda)$ from the curve for $F(\lambda)$, and $\delta'(\lambda)$ and $\delta_0'(\lambda)$ are found in an exactly similar way from the curves for $\delta(\lambda)$ and $\delta_0(\lambda)$.

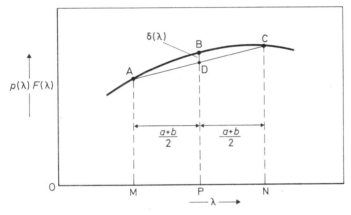

Fig. 25. Slit-width correction in spectrophotometry (after Walsh, 1958).

It should be noticed that $\delta(\lambda)$ is positive when the curve is convex towards the λ-axis (that is, it is negative in Fig. 25). When $a = b$ the expression reduces to

$$\frac{\phi(\lambda)}{f(\lambda)} = \frac{(p(\lambda)F(\lambda)-\delta(\lambda)/12+\delta'(\lambda)/90-...)}{(F(\lambda)-\delta_0(\lambda)/12+\delta_0'(\lambda)/90-...)}$$

$F(\lambda)$ may be calculated from $f(\lambda)$ if the dispersion curve of the prism is known, for $F(\lambda)$ is proportional to $V_\lambda f(\lambda)/\Delta(\lambda)$, where $\Delta(\lambda)$ represents the dispersion and V_λ the relative luminous efficiency of radiation. More complex treatments have been developed by Hardy and Young (1949) Eberhardt (1950) and Brodersen (1954). Of these the method of Hardy and Young is most quantitatively precise, that of Eberhardt is most useful for providing analytic expressions and that of Brodersen (drawing on his earlier experience (Brodersen, 1953) with infra-red spectroscopes) the most practically applicable.

7.1.2.   *Stray light*

Another form of contribution to the non-monochromaticity of the monochromator output is stray light, which may be defined as energy transmitted outside the desired pass band (the limits of which will have been set by considerations of instrument design, of the type discussed in the previous section).

The importance of identifying and eliminating the causes of stray light cannot be overemphasized—if a white light source is being used the desired wavelength radiation may constitute only a small fraction of the source output and the signal would be extremely susceptible to swamping at the detector by broad-spectrum stray light. This is particularly so if the detector itself has an unusual spectral response curve (the eye, for instance, observing in the blue would find great difficulty in discriminating against stray green light).

The worst effects of stray light may be removed by using relatively broad band filters at the monochromator exit slit, but for convenient measurement a continuous filter, from blue to red, of the type proposed by Crawford and Marsh (1957) would be required. Thus it is necessary to consider how this effect arises and how it may be minimized.

The chief sources of stray light are:

1. Multiple reflections between optical elements
2. Surface diffusion from flaws, scratches or dirt on the optical elements
3. Fluorescence of elements within the monochromator.

It is assumed that no stray light enters due to faulty construction of the monochromator housing.

Multiple reflections. At any refracting surface most of the incident radiation will be transmitted but a proportion (0·04 at normal incidence, increasing with angle) will be reflected. Because of reflections of this type, each lens in the system will give rise to a number of spurious images as shown in Fig. 26. A first attempt at eliminating these images might be the provision of thin-film anti-reflection coatings (blooming) on the lens surfaces. This, however, is only effective for selected wavelengths and is at best a limited solution. Most monochromators use light baffles or 'stops' as internal screens along the ray path in an attempt to reduce this effect. There are other approaches incorporated in specific instruments to be considered later.

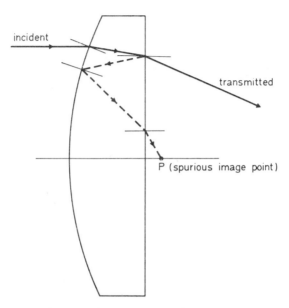

FIG. 26. Spurious image formation.

Surface diffusion. If the components have been well made, diffusion from actual surface defects should be negligible. However, this is not true of diffusion from surface contamination by dust or other particles. It is not always possible to seal a system permanently and in that case the interior should be made permanently tacky to prevent the circulation of particles.

In assessing the importance of this effect the obvious step is to relate it to the number of optical surfaces in the system. This is not, however, strictly valid since diffusion from surfaces at or near the slits is a minimal effect tending to broaden the slit at the scattering intensity; diffusion from surfaces near the prism is correspondingly more important. Since it is difficult to quantify this positional importance it is easier to accept the simple criterion of number of optical surfaces as the important factor. This number should thus be kept to the minimum compatible with the efficient operation of the instrument.

Fluorescence. When light is absorbed by a substance its energy may be transformed in various ways. One of these ways is for it to be re-emitted as fluorescence radiation. Generally, atoms excited by the absorbed light energy are de-activated by collision with consequent re-emission of the radiation. In the case of fluorescence radiation, however, the emission comes from complex molecules which seem to be shielded from external influences and, thereby, de-activation. The wavelength of the fluorescent light is, according to Stokes's law, longer than that of the absorbed light and it is emitted isotropically.

The magnitude of the fluorescence is generally small (Rodriguez *et al.*, 1943) but is, in any case, dependent on the constituent materials of the glass used in the monochromator. Thus its minimization is a matter of judicious choice.

An elegant method of eliminating stray light was used by W. D. Wright (1954) in designing his spectrophotometer. Besides the provision of stops and screening along the optical path the waveband selected from the spectrum is returned by a narrow mirror to retraverse the dispersing elements. The mirror is slightly angled so that the return beam is lower than the primary one and so may be conveniently directed out of the system after passing through the prisms. The elimination of the stray light occurs at the exit slit of the first monochromator (the mirror), which is also the entrance slit of a 'second' monochromator. The instrument is thus effectively a double monochromator and the stray light is efficiently screened out by the succession of slits.

A simple test which may be performed to test the efficacy, or otherwise, of the methods chosen to eliminate stray light was suggested by Crawford. A narrow-band interference filter is used to cut out the stray light at a selected frequency and the detected signal is compared to that from the unfiltered beam.

Other methods have been proposed by Pritchard (1955) and Preston (1936). Pritchard used a quasi-monochromatic source of known characteristics so that stray light generated by passage through the instrument could be expressed as an output/input ratio. Preston's method—extremely tedious and of little practical use, except for checking—involved the use of complementary screens at the entrance and exit slits of the monochromator under test with a series of readings to be taken for various permutations of screen positions.

7.2. REFLECTOMETERS

The reflection characteristics of specular surfaces are a function of the angle of the incident radiation. Thus a standard method of specifying a surface's characteristics is to plot a graph of reflectance as a function of angle of incidence. Consequently it is a requirement of the measuring instrument that there should be a facility for allowing measurements to be made at all angles between 0° and 90°.

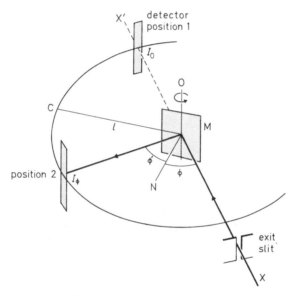

FIG. 27. Schematic diagram of a reflectometer.

To prevent photometric errors caused by imperfect collimation of the measuring beam, the detector and the specimen must be mounted to rotate coaxially (so that the detector is always a fixed distance from the exit slit).

Fig. 27 shows the general arrangement of a specimen/detector system, which may be referred to as the reflectometer attachment for the monochromator source.

XX' is the optical axis and O is the common axis of rotation of the mirror surface M and the detector. The detector will describe a circle C of radius l, the radius of the outer case. N is the mirror normal, ϕ is the angle of incidence and ϕ' the angle of reflection.

The sensitive area of the detector is shown to be rectangular and is big enough to receive all the incident energy.

Radiation from a monochromator, the exit slit of which is shown, travels along XX′ to M and is reflected to the detector at position 2. The detector signal is proportional to the intensity of the reflected radiation I_ϕ at that particular angle of incidence. If absolute values of $\mathscr{R}$ are desired, rather than relative values, the mirror is moved out of the beam and the detector swung round to position 1, so that the incident intensity I_0 can be measured. Angles of incidence are measured with respect to XX′ with $\phi = 90°$ (grazing incidence) occurring when the detector is in position 2. Usually the detector is free to move to any position on the circle but the finite widths of the radiation beam and mirror prevent making measurements very close to grazing incidence because the mirror may not intercept all the beam. In addition the finite size of the detector prevents measurements close to normal incidence since the detector will then eclipse the radiation emerging from the exit slit.

The motions of the mirror and detector may be independent or coupled. In the first case the measurement is made by setting either the detector or mirror at the desired angle and rotating the other until the maximum signal is obtained. In the second case, coupling is accomplished by using an angle divider such that the mirror rotation is half that of the detector. The reflected beam then always falls on the detector and it is not necessary to find the maximum signal, which might be difficult if the signal is noisy.

7.3. REFLECTOMETRY ERRORS

W. R. Hunter (1967) has considered the errors involved in the use of a system such as the one just described, and groups them under the headings of mechanical, optical and miscellaneous.

7.3.1. *Mechanical*

Reflectance errors caused by inaccurate measurements of ϕ are proportional to $\Delta\mathscr{R}/\Delta\phi$ which can be calculated if n and k are known explicitly. If, however, the measurements are to determine n and k (see § 9.1) then the error must be assessed empirically.

This type of error occurs if specimen and detector are not coaxial (Fig. 28). Two methods may be used to eliminate the error. The most obvious one is to adjust the position of the specimen along its normal so that M passes through O. If no adjustment is possible then a detector is required with a uniformly sensitive area large enough to receive the radiation reflected to A' when it is farthest removed from A. The first method would appear to

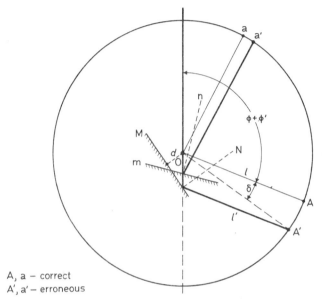

A, a – correct
A', a' – erroneous

FIG. 28. Effect of the displacement error on reflectance measurement.

be better owing to the difficulty of obtaining large-area detectors with uniform response.

A second possibility for error lies in the non-coincidence of the optical axis XX' and the optical axis of the monochromator to which the reflectometer is attached. This mechanical deviation error (MDE) cannot be eliminated merely by using a detector with a large uniformly sensitive surface, or by independent settings of the mirror and detector since an incorrect value of ϕ is involved. Furthermore the magnitude of the error in determining ϕ is independent of ϕ so it is not easily determined experimentally. This error may be compensated by averaging the corresponding reflectances measured on both sides of XX' because the sign of the error depends on the orientation of the mirror with respect to XX'—equal angles of incidence on opposite sides of XX' have angular errors of equal magnitude and opposite sign. This method is only effective for small deviation errors.

7.3.2. *Optical*

A non-uniform spatial distribution of intensity in the radiation beam emerging from the monochromator causes the centre of gravity of the beam to be displaced from XX' and will have the same effect as misalignment of the optic axes even though the mechanical alignment may be within tolerance. Hunter refers to this as the optical deviation error (ODE).

Non-uniform illumination can cause a more serious error in measuring reflectance if the detector sensitivity varies over its surface. If, for example, a non-uniform beam were reversed, the signal from a non-uniform detector would change. Such a reversal in the plane of incidence occurs on reflection when the detector moves from the position where I_0 is measured to any position where the reflected beam is measured.

A separate source of error caused by detector non-uniformity occurs, if there is displacement error, as the angle of incidence changes. Because of the relative motion between the detector and the position at which the reflected beam intersects the detector circle, different parts of the detector are illuminated as ϕ changes, consequently the reflected beam signal will be modulated by the detector sensitivity function. This type of error can occur even when the beam is uniform. Attempts have been made to eliminate the effect by coating the glass envelope of the detector with a dispersive film (Johnson *et al.*, 1951).

Non-linearity of the detector will cause errors in the measured reflectance. In the case of photomultipliers, non-linearity can arise from:

1. The external circuit of the multiplier

2. Conditions within the tube (charge accumulation on insulating supports)

3. Space-charge accumulation in the last stages when the radiation is very intense.

Another possible source of error in reflectance measurements associated with the detector is its sensitivity to polarization. Even though the radiation incident on the mirror may be unpolarized, that reflected from the mirror will be polarized to a degree depending on n, k and ϕ. Hence if the detector is sensitive to polarization the resulting reflectance values may not be correct. The effects of polarization can be eliminated by taking measurements at two azimuth settings of the reflectometer 90° apart and averaging them.

In most reflectance studies the effect of scattering of the incident radiation is ignored—it is assumed that the reflection surface is smooth. However, in the spectral region where the wavelength is no longer much larger than the surface irregularities, scattering may account for an appreciable amount of the radiation leaving the surface, and the specularly reflected intensity will appear less than that predicted by the Fresnel formulae. Attempts have been made to calculate the magnitude of this effect using the Kirchhoff methods mentioned in Part 1 (see Bennett and Porteus, 1961). Practical measurements of the optical constants of evaporated iridium films at 0·03 μ indicate that the simple theory predicts greater scattering than actually occurs (Hass *et al.*, 1967). This error is probably due, in part, to the use of Gaussian statistics to describe the surface, and partly to the use of scalar scattering theory. However, the simple theory successfully predicts the increase in scattering with decreasing angle of incidence which is characteristic of scattering surfaces.

7.3.3. *Miscellaneous*

Fluctuations in intensity of the radiation emerging from the monochromator, and in the gain of the photomultiplier, and associated electronics, will also cause errors in reflectance measurements. Rapid fluctuations in radiation intensity, with periods of 0·1 s and less, seldom cause much trouble because the time constant of the electronics used to process the photomultiplier signal can be adjusted to average the fluctuations. By the same method, noise from the photomultiplier can be reduced. More serious problems are caused by slow fluctuations, or drifts in the incident radiation intensity, and in the gains of the photo-multiplier and electronics. These, however, are primarily electronic problems and will not be considered further.

8

Reflectometer Techniques

In previous sections the quantity termed specular reflectance was defined practically, and a description given of an instrument by which it might be measured. Instruments very similar to the design outlined have been built and used successfully by a number of workers, notably W. D. Wright (1954) and W. R. Hunter (1967).

However, there have been other approaches to the problem, usually necessitated by a particular interest in measuring one or two specific conditions.

8.1. NEAR-NORMAL INCIDENCE

In determining the reflectance of materials there are several important advantages to be gained by working at near-normal incidence; the reflectance at zero incidence is a comparatively simple function of the optical constants n and k of the materials involved; the reflectance is insensitive to polarization effects, thus the polarization introduced by the monochromator and auxiliary optics does not affect the accuracy of the measurements; the angle of incidence is not critical—if the angle of incidence is chosen sufficiently near zero the values of the reflectance co-efficients for the two states of polarization $\mathcal{R}_p$ and $\mathcal{R}_s$ will differ from $\mathcal{R}$ by an amount less than the precision of the measurement.

These advantages have been rather difficult to realize because of the difficulties of working at normal, or near-normal, incidence. If an instrument of the type already described is operated at these angles, then, in addition to errors arising from inadequate measuring precision, there may be various systematic errors in the measured reflectance. The major sources of *optical* systematic errors are:

1. Variation of image position on the detector face due to tilt or displacement of the sample.

2. Use of a reference mirror (depends very much on the accuracy with which the absolute reflectance of the reference mirror is known).

3. The optical path lengths corresponding to sample measurement and signal measurement are not identical (particularly true for multiple-reflection methods).

With these advantages and difficulties in mind we may consider some attempts on the problem.

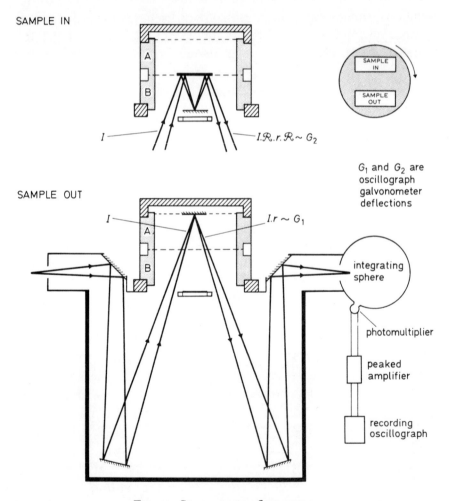

FIG. 29. Strong-type reflectometer.

Bennett and Koehler (1960) used a Strong-type reflectometer (Strong, 1938, p. 376) for their work in the visible region. Fig. 29 shows a sketch of the apparatus. The absolute reflectance was obtained using the relation

$$\mathcal{R} = \sqrt{(G_2/G_1)}.$$

The average angle of incidence on the sample in the instrument was 7°. The two conditions 'sample in' and 'sample out' are obtained by rotating a cylinder through 180°. Since the cylinder comprises two identical blocks, A and B, either of which may be placed on top of the other, four different orientations of the blocks are possible. By taking products of the ratios measured in various orientations of A and B, the absolute specular reflectance of the sample may be obtained even if the reflectances, r, of the small mirrors mounted on the two blocks are not exactly equal. A 300-cycle light chopper and a Hilger-Mueller fused quartz double monochromator were used ahead of the reflectometer.

The method of Bennett and Koehler gives a direct measure of the square of the reflectance and this results in improved accuracy for high reflectance values but less accuracy for low values. Shaw and Blevin (1964) describe an absolute reflectometer for measuring with *normally* incident flux the direct spectral reflectances of optically flat surfaces. Though simple, (Fig. 30), high accuracy is claimed.

Clear silica plates, P_1 and P_2 are used to direct towards the photocell the fraction of the flux reflected by the sample (sample in) and the flux incident (sample out) respectively. The mirror M_2 images the aperture of the monochromator prisms within aperture A_1 and images the exit slit S at the front of the photocell, the linear magnification being three in the latter case. Two laterally separated images of the slit are formed by reflection at both surfaces of the plate P_1. Only the flux reflected by the inner surface of P_1 (nearer the sample) is passed by the aperture A_2 and measured. This is ensured by making plate P_1 thick enough to separate the two slit images by about 1 cm. The plate P_2 is similarly arranged.

With measurements required of the reflectance $\mathcal{R}$, let r_1 and r_2 be the reflectances of the inner surfaces of P_1 and P_2 respectively for 40° incidence and for the state of polarization of the incident light. With unit flux incident on the sample, the flux F_R in the P_1 beam is

$$F_R = \mathcal{R}r_1$$

With the sample removed, the flux F_1 in the right beam is given by

$$F_1 = r_2$$

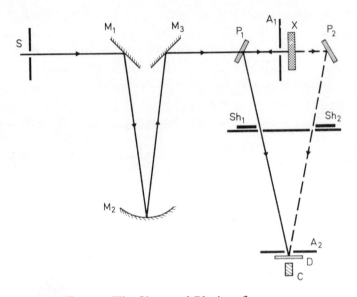

FIG. 30. The Shaw and Blevin reflectometer.

M_1, M_3 Plane mirrors. Sh_1, Sh_2 Shutters.
M_2 Spherical mirror.   D   Diffuser.
P_1, P_2 Silica plates.   C   Photocell.

The ratio F_R/F_1 gives the reflectance immediately provided that r_1 and r_2 are equal. If they are not then

$$F_R/F_1 = \mathcal{R}r_1/r_2$$

and it is necessary to repeat the measurements with P_1 and P_2 interchanged. This gives $\mathcal{R}r_2/r_1$ and the reflectance $\mathcal{R}$ may then be found.

   The reflectometer enabled absolute measurements of direct spectral reflectance to be made to an accuracy of about ± 0.1 per cent in the wavelength range of 0.2–2.5 μ.

8.2. REFLECTANCE IN THE ULTRA-VIOLET

Radiation measurements in the air absorption region of the spectrum, which begins at about 0·18 μ and extends to X-rays are usually performed in a vacuum chamber. Smith (1960) describes an instrument for this sort of application. One feature of it is that the detector is located outside the vacuum. This eliminates the possibility of glow discharge between the photo-cathode and any nearby grounded surface, which can occur for

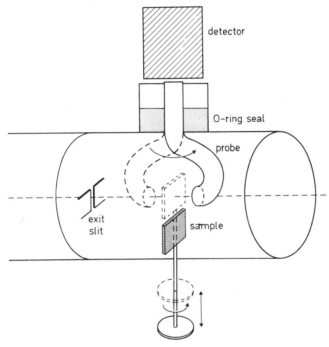

FIG. 31. The Smith reflectometer.

certain low-pressure ranges. It further allows the reflectometer chamber to be compact and permits placement of the sample quite close to the exit slit, thus reducing the necessary size of the sample.

A glass probe (Fig. 31) is the principal element of the device. The probe is a pyrex rod bent to the shape indicated and polished at both ends. The entrance end of the probe is coated with a phosphor, sodium salicylate. In the presence of ultra-violet radiation, the phosphor fluoresces at approximately 0·4 μ.

Although the probe will not transmit ultra-violet radiation below about 0·3 μ it will readily transmit the 0·4 μ fluorescence. Since the phosphor acts as a diffuse source, the walls of the probe are coated with aluminium in order to contain that radiation incident at less than the critical angle.

An O-ring seals all but the end of the probe in the vacuum. The end-on photomultiplier is mounted outside the system with the photocathode as close as possible to the end of the probe. Reflectance measurements are made by comparing the signals piped up the probe for the sample-in and sample-out positions in the normal way. Minimum angle of incidence is limited by the position at which the probe, when intercepting the reflected beam, begins to obscure the incident beam. Maximum angle of incidence is limited by the width of the sample. Angle of incidence is determined by scales which are etched on the adjustment rings for the probe and the sample.

A more rudimentary approach to measurements in the ultra-violet, with considerably less scope, was reported by Purcell (1953). His method does not require working in a vacuum, instead it makes use of four narrow atmospheric transmission bands in the region 0·114 μ to 0·119 μ. The source used was a hydrogen arc with a lithium fluoride window and the detector was a thermo-luminescent phosphor (manganese-activated calcium sulphate).

8.3. REFLECTANCE IN THE INFRA-RED

It is possible, in principle, to make measurements in the infra-red region on most instruments and it is generally other factors which dictate changes to the basic instrument.

Bennett and Koehler (1960) wishing to obtain precise absolute reflectance values in the infra-red found that they could not do this with the apparatus described in § 8.1. The design they chose is shown in Fig. 32. The average angle of incidence on the sample is 5°. The sample at S is mounted in a vertical slide and can be taken out of the beam. Fig. 33 illustrates a unique compensating feature of the optical design. The solid lines represent the path of a ray when the sample is correctly positioned. The dotted line is the path when the sample is displaced. The focusing property of the mirror M_8 (which has a focal range larger than the

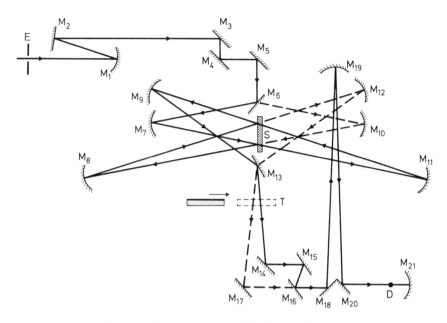

FIG. 32. The Bennett and Koehler reflectometer.

E   Exit slit of monochromator.
S   Reflectance position of sample.
T   Transmission position of sample.
D   Detector.
M_1–M_{21} Mirrors.

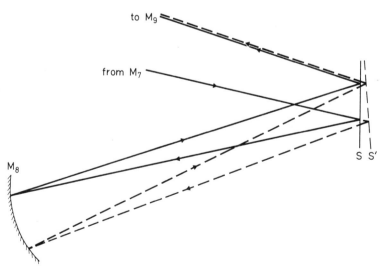

FIG. 33. Sample-tilt compensation.

maximum sample displacement) means that the rays to M_9 actually coincide.

A lot of spectrophotometry in the infra-red is devoted to determining the optical constants of the reflecting material (see § 9.1). In order to do this it is necessary to use polarized light in the instrument. Fig. 34 shows the rather unusual source-detector configuration chosen by Oldham (1951) for these measurements; the reflected beam is eventually focused on the entrance slit of the spectrometer for analysis rather than the other way round.

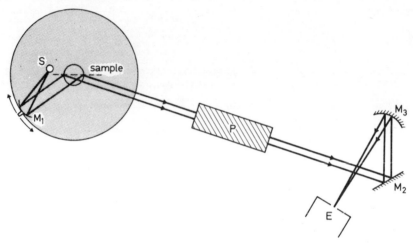

FIG. 34. The Oldham reflectometer.

P   Polarizer.
S   Source.
E   Entrance slit.
M_1, M_3 Spherical mirrors.
M_2 Plane mirror.

The determination of optical constants in the infra-red was also considered by Conn and Eaton (1954) and Swindell (1968), using a rotating polarizer. With the reflected light being examined by an analyser the intensity was modulated at twice the frequency of rotation of the polarizer. The resultant signal vanishes at the tuning condition $\bar{\phi}$, $\bar{\psi}$ (principal angle of incidence, principal azimuth) and these quantities are directly related to the optical constants.

Other measurement methods by Gier *et al.* (1954) and Reid and McAlister (1959) are mainly of use for the measurement of diffuse infra-red reflectance.

8.4. LOW TEMPERATURES

Weeks (1958), in the course of a study of the luminescence of alkali iodides, found it necessary to measure the absolute specular reflectance, as a function of wavelength, of single crystals at liquid nitrogen temperatures. As shown in Fig. 35, the crystal is

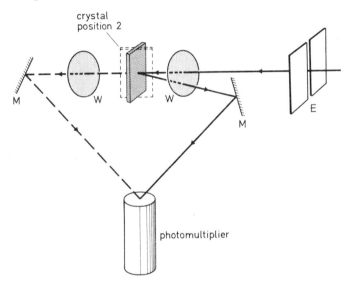

FIG. 35. The Weeks reflectometer.

    E   Exit slit of monochromator.
    W   Window
    M   Mirror (positions 1 and 2).

mounted slightly off axis on the rotating cooling block of the cryostat. It is placed at the required angle of incidence to the beam from the monochromator by rotating the cooling block. Since the crystal is off axis it may also be moved out of the beam. A mirror and photomultiplier are mounted outside of the cryostat so that they can be rotated independently about the cooling-tube axis. Two readings are taken: one with the crystal rotated out of the beam, and one with it rotated to intercept the beam at the required angle of incidence (the mirror and photomultiplier are also rotated to catch the reflected beam). Hence the reflectance can be measured.

This system has the advantage that the measured reflectance is independent of the spectral response of the detector and the reflectivity of the mirror and windows. When used at oblique incidence, both the p- and s-components of reflectance can be measured independently by suitably polarizing the incident beam.

Hartman and Logothetis (1964) developed a reflectometer very similar to the one described but constructed it so that the unit could be installed in the specimen compartment of a Cary-14 recording spectrophotometer.

8.5.   ILLUMINATING ENGINEERING

All of the instruments and techniques considered so far have strictly speaking been applicable only to laboratory measurement. The illuminating engineer, however, demands a facility for measuring reflectance in normal environmental conditions. The dimensions of this problem indicate not a single instrument but separate, or separable, source and detector.

A comprehensive report on the evaluation of the effects of interior lighting has been published by Blackwell (1967). The source (or sources) was normal room lighting and its efficiency

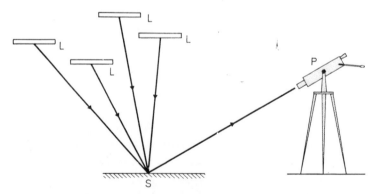

FIG. 36. Interior lighting photometry.

L   Luminaire.
P   Photometer.
S   Specimen surface.

was assessed in terms of defined quantities of contrast and level of illumination for people performing specific tasks (reading, writing, working). Measurements were made with a Pritchard tele-photometer which could be located in positions simulating the observer's eye (Fig. 36). The overall conditions of measurement corresponded to the hemispherical-directional situation described in § 6.3. Thus there was no absolute measurement of specular reflectance, only indications, depending on the test surface, at the specular angle to particular luminaires.

Similar arrangements are used for studies of the efficiency of outdoor lighting systems.

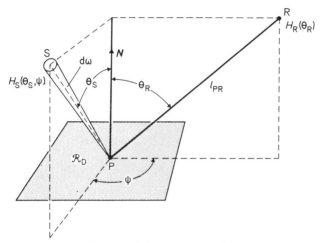

FIG. 37. Reflectance notation.

8.6. ABSOLUTE MEASUREMENT

In considering the instruments and techniques of measuring specular reflectance it is apparent that the values obtained are strictly valid only for the particular instrument's operating conditions as defined in chapter 6. It would be desirable, there-fore, if there were simple procedures by which measurements might be made independent of the exact viewing and illuminating conditions.

Such procedures have, in fact, been suggested by Spencer and Gray (1960). Using the terms defined in Fig. 37 they derived the relation for specular/diffuse reflectance:

$$H_R(\theta_R) = \exp(-\alpha l_{PR}) \{\pi^{-1} \int \mathscr{R}_D(\theta_R;\theta_S,\Psi) \cos \theta_S H_S(\theta_S,\Psi) \, d\omega$$
$$+ \mathscr{R}(\theta_R)H_S(\theta_R,\pi)\}$$

where

H_R is the brightness at R
H_S is the source brightness (measured at P)
α is attenuation coefficient of viewing medium
l_{PR} is viewing distance from sample
$\mathscr{R}$ is the specular reflectance
$\mathscr{R}_D$ is the diffuse reflectance.

Thus in general the diffuse reflectance is a function of the three angles θ_R, θ_S and Ψ. The specular reflectance is a function of only one.

The procedures for measuring an absolute value of $\mathscr{R}$ arise from the equation. For a single source of light subtending a small solid angle at P (and appearing uniform as viewed from P):

$$\frac{H_R(\theta_R)}{H_S(\theta_{R'}\,\pi)} = \frac{\cos\theta_R}{\pi}\,\mathscr{R}_D(\theta_R;\theta_R,\pi)\,\omega + \mathscr{R}(\theta_R)$$

If H_R/H_S is measured as a function of ω for a succession of small solid angles then in the limit, as ω becomes very small, the curve approaches a straight line as shown in Fig. 38. The intercept with the vertical axis is $\mathscr{R}$. The slope is $\{(\cos\theta_R)/\pi\}\mathscr{R}_D$.

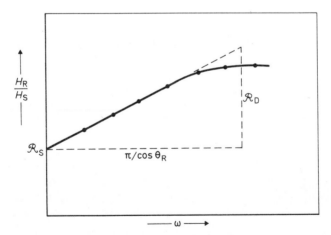

FIG. 38. (H_R/H_S) as a function of ω (after Spencer and Gray, 1960).

In order to resolve the specular and diffuse components at the specular angle three conditions must be satisfied.

1. The source of light must appear uniform as viewed by sample and receiver

2. The diameter of the uniform source of light must be variable

3. For the most accurate determination of the specular reflectance, as well as the simplest form of equations, the source must be large enough to fill the entire field of view of the receiver.

8.7. GLOSSMETERS

Whilst the main concern has been to identify and measure the uniquely specular component of reflection it is nevertheless desirable for certain purposes to obtain a rough measure of the light reflected within a certain solid angle including the specular direction. Such measurements are made with instruments known as 'glossmeters' and the values obtained, although arbitrary, are comparable with one another so long as the same instrument is used. They are needed for such purposes as the control of the calendering process in paper manufacture, the description of the surface finish in paints or enamels, and so on.

One of the earliest instruments was the Ingersoll Glarimeter (Ingersoll, 1921) which depended on the fact that specularly reflected light is almost completely polarized in the plane of incidence, while that diffusely reflected is unpolarized (see Part 1). Light from a source (Fig. 39) subtending a certain small solid angle (approximately 0·038 steradian) illuminates the test surface at T_2, the light being incident at an angle of about 57·5° (the Brewster angle for paper). The Wollaston prism W gives a double image of the slit S and is so set that the specularly reflected light is completely extinguished in one image. The Nicol prism N is rotated until the two images are of equal brightness. In this case if A is the angle of rotation of the Nicol, while D and S are the intensities of the diffuse and specular components within the angle of acceptance of the instrument,

$$\tfrac{1}{2}D/(\tfrac{1}{2}D+S) = \tan^2 A$$

or

$$S/(D+S) = \cos 2A$$

So that, of the light forming the images viewed in the eyepiece, the fraction that is specularly reflected is cos $2A$.

Since this early instrument, the design principles have changed little, most new instruments offering only a little more scope,

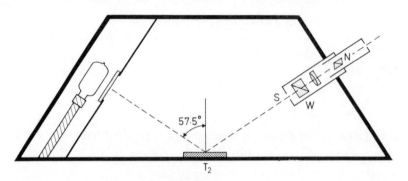

FIG. 39. The Ingersoll Glarimeter.

N   Nicol prism.
W   Wollaston prism.
S   Slit.
T_2 Point on test surface.

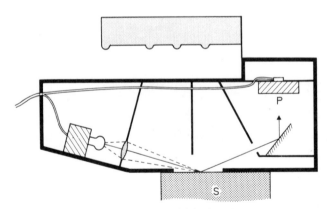

FIG. 40. The Hunter glossmeter.
S   Surface.   P   Detector.

speed or convenience. After having worked on this type of instrument for some years, R. S. Hunter (1940) developed a multi-purpose reflectometer. This was notable for its facility for measuring, amongst other things, specular gloss, trichromatic coefficients and apparent reflectance. Detection was by two photo-

good linearity. Gloss values in ASTM units are read directly from a counter dial to the nearest o·1 unit.

With the extensive use of chrome and polished metal trim on cars, manufacturers wished to be able to quantify the metallic appearance of a particular finish (see § 9.3). Barkman (1959) proposed a measurement of metallic brightness using an integrating sphere to separate diffuse and specular reflection. An optical

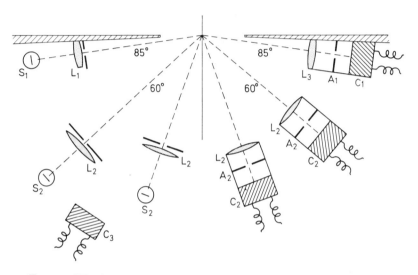

FIG. 42. The Schreckendgust and Gowing direct-reading glossmeter.

S_1, S_2 G.E. prefocused light sources.
L_1 Triplet lens.
L_2, L_3 Double convex lenses.
C_1, C_2, C_3 Photocells.
A_1, A_2 Adjustable apertures.

diagram of a sphere photometer is shown in Fig. 43. All light reflected within ± 4° of the specular direction is considered to be specular. To measure total reflectance, either the incident light beam or the sphere is rotated to trap the specular beam in the sphere.

Further work on glossmeters for the specific investigation of metallic brightness led to the DORI meter of Tingle and Potter (1961), in which the distinctness-of-image gloss was measured by the amount of light reaching a single receptor slit relative to that received by the same slit when positioned in the centre of one of the source images. Tingle and George (1965) described a companion instrument to the DORI meter which was essentially an abridged goniophotometer (Fig. 44). It had a single fixed incident beam and an adjustable receptor assembly so constructed

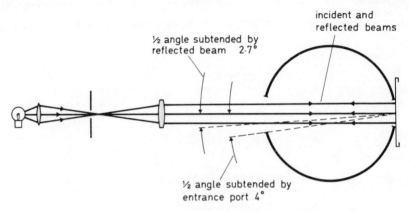

SPECULAR-EXCLUDED POSITION: INCIDENT BEAM AT 0°

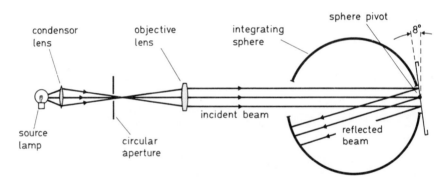

SPECULAR-INCLUDED POSITION: INCIDENT BEAM AT 8°

FIG. 43. Diagram of the D25P sphere optical unit.

that the amount of light at angles 2, 5, 10, 15, and 20° from the specular centre-line could be measured relative to the intensity of the specular beam.

The success of these two instruments prompted Christie (1969) to develop an instrument combining the most desirable features of both, the Hunterlab D-47 DORI-Gon glossmeter (Fig. 45). In a description of the instrument Christie compared it

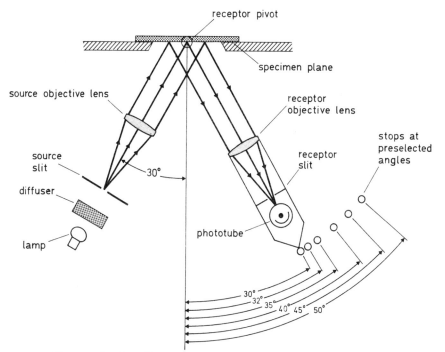

FIG. 44. Optical diagram of the Alcoa abridged goniophotometer.

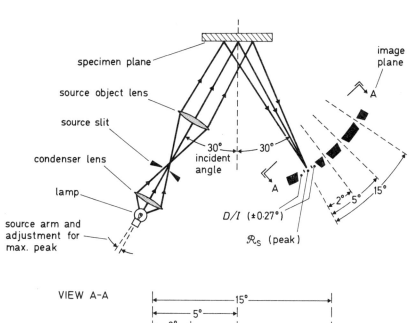

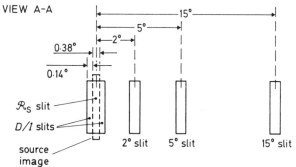

FIG. 45. Optical diagram of the D-47 Dori-Gon glossmeter.

with four other different designs previously used for metallic appearance evaluation. On a simple ranking comparison, excellent correlation was found between the results from the instruments as well as between these results and visual judgements.

8.8 POLYNOMIAL REPRESENTATION OF REFLECTANCE CURVES

Bridgeman (1961), describing his investigations into the possibility of forecasting the concentrations of pigments required to produce a paint of any desired colour, noted that there is a stage in the calculation at which spectral reflectances are converted into tri-stimulus values by evaluating certain integrals of the form

$$\int \mathscr{R}(\lambda)J(\lambda)\,d\lambda$$

This integral had traditionally been evaluated by replacing it by the sum $\Sigma\,\mathscr{R}(\lambda_i)J(\lambda_i)$ taken over n wavelengths λ_i (n was generally taken as 30 or 32). This was thus, essentially, an n-point trapezoidal rule for numerical integration. The object of Bridgeman's paper was to show that, provided the calculated spectral reflectance curves had certain general characteristics, then a more powerful method of numerical integration using fewer points (25) could be utilized.

A more elegant approach to this problem, and one which had been foreseen by Bouguer (1961) in the eighteenth century, was suggested by Moon and Spencer (1945b). They considered the possibility of replacing the reflectance parameter with its polynomial representation. They did this by examining over 600 reflectance curves and classifying them into six types (Fig. 46). In their notation:

Type I is approximated by the equation

$$\mathscr{R}(\lambda) = A + B\lambda \tag{8.1}$$

Type II makes use of the equation

$$\mathscr{R}(\lambda) = A + B\lambda^m \tag{8.2}$$

The characteristic shape for the reflectance curve of white materials (Type III) is represented by

$$\mathscr{R}(\lambda) = A - B\lambda^{-m} \tag{8.3}$$

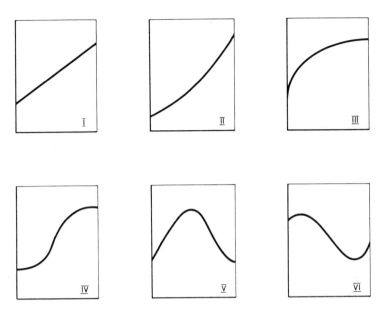

FIG. 46. Six types of reflectance curves (after Moon and Spencer, 1945b).

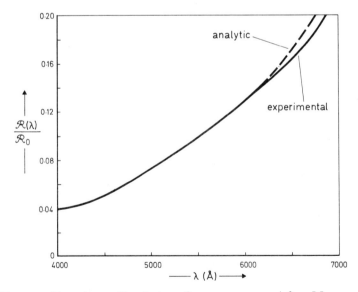

FIG. 47. Experimental/analytic reflectance curves (after Moon and Spencer, 1945b). Material—Masonite wall board. For the analytic curve, $m = 6$ in equation (8.2).

The remaining types are covered by a polynomial of the form

$$\mathscr{R}(\lambda) = K_0 + K_1\lambda + K_2\lambda^2 + \ldots + K_6\lambda^6 \qquad (8.4)$$

All of these equations may be extended by correction terms.

Moon and Spencer show examples of the accuracy of their method. Fig. 47 compares the curve drawn by a Hardy photoelectric spectrophotometer with the broken line representing the plotting of the equation

$$\mathscr{R}(\lambda)/\mathscr{R}_0 = 0.0388 + 1.466\lambda^6 \qquad (8.5)$$

When the shape of the curve does not give an obvious indication of its mathematical approximation it is possible to obtain the coefficients from the relation

$$K_m = \sum_{k=0}^{6} C_m^k \mathscr{R}(\lambda_k) \qquad (8.6)$$

$$m = 0, 1, 2, 3, \ldots, 6$$

$$\lambda_0, \ldots, \lambda_6 = 0.4\,\mu, \ldots, 0.7\,\mu$$

The constants C_m^k have been evaluated and are available in table form (Moon and Spencer, 1945b).

Moon and Spencer (1945a) give examples of the type of functions suitable for this treatment and refer to their previous work on the subject. Although many reflectance curves may be represented by simple polynomials of the sort discussed there are other curves which cannot be adequately expressed in this way and which must be handled by numerical computation.

9

Applications of Reflectance
Data

In Part 1 of this monograph, specular reflectance was defined in terms of the optical constants of reflecting materials and, to a certain extent, their surface structure. It is reasonable then to propose that measurements of the specular reflectance under appropriate conditions will enable these surface properties to be computed.

Other applications of a detailed knowledge of reflection properties can vary from optical system design to ascribing a degree of obtrusiveness to a factory in a rural landscape.

9.1. DETERMINATION OF OPTICAL CONSTANTS

A number of experimental methods have been devised to determine optical constants, the refractive index n, and the extinction coefficient k, by means of reflectance measurements. Humphreys-Owen (1961) lists nine reflection methods based on the use of reflectances with p-polarized, s-polarized and unpolarized light ($\mathscr{R}_p$, $\mathscr{R}_s$, and $\mathscr{R}$ respectively). From these reflectances and known angles of incidence various pairs of measurements are chosen— a particular pair of measurements represents a method. The list runs

Class 1. One reflectance measurement at two angles of incidence.

Method	*Reflectance measured*
A	$\mathscr{R}$
B	$\mathscr{R}_p$
C	$\mathscr{R}_s$
D	$\mathscr{R}_p/\mathscr{R}_s$

79

or   Two reflectance measurements at one angle of incidence
     E $\mathcal{R}_p$ and $\mathcal{R}_s$ separately.

Class 2. One reflectance measurement at any angle and measure-
            ment of a special angle having an optical property which
            supplies the necessary second condition (usually the
            Brewster angle).

Method	*Reflectance measured*
F	$\mathcal{R}_p$ at Brewster angle
G	$\mathcal{R}_s$ at Brewster angle
H	$\mathcal{R}_p/\mathcal{R}_s$ at Brewster angle
J	either $\mathcal{R}_p$, $\mathcal{R}_s$, or $\mathcal{R}_p/\mathcal{R}_s$ at any other angle.

Of these nine methods the so-called '$\mathcal{R}$ versus ϕ' seems the most generally applied. $\mathcal{R}$ is measured for two or more angles of incidence, ϕ, and the generalized Fresnel formulae connecting $\mathcal{R}$ with n, k and ϕ are solved for n and k. Since the equations cannot be solved explicitly, various methods have been proposed to obtain working solutions. All are essentially the same since they represent simultaneous solution of the Fresnel equations and involve a graphical procedure. W. R. Hunter (1965), considering the method and associated errors, explains one manner in which it may be applied.

A number of curves of $\mathcal{R}$ as a function of n for constant values of k and for a particular angle of incidence, are plotted using values calculated from the Fresnel equations (Fig. 48). The case illustrated shows the results for 20° angle of incidence. Suppose that the measured value of $\mathcal{R}$ for 20° is 30 per cent, as shown by the heavy horizontal line. This value of $\mathcal{R}$ corresponds to many pairs of n and k which when plotted in the n–k plane (Fig. 49) give the iso-reflectance curve for 20°, shown by the heavy line labelled 20°. Similarly a reflectance measurement of another angle of incidence would prove a second iso-reflectance curve and the intersection with the first curve would be the solution for n and k. In practice there is seldom a common point of intersection; this is shown in Fig. 49. When there is no common intersection the centre of gravity of the figure formed by the intersecting curves is taken as the solution. A separate calculation of $\mathcal{R}$ versus ϕ should then be performed to verify that the best centre was chosen.

In his consideration of the errors of this method Hunter chose the angle of intersection of the iso-reflectance curves as his parameter of sensitivity because this is the factor which determines the change in location of the intersection for a given error in the measurement.

In his analysis, Hunter broadened his terms of reference to include the reflectances $\mathscr{R}_p$ and $\mathscr{R}_s$ for p- and s-polarized incident

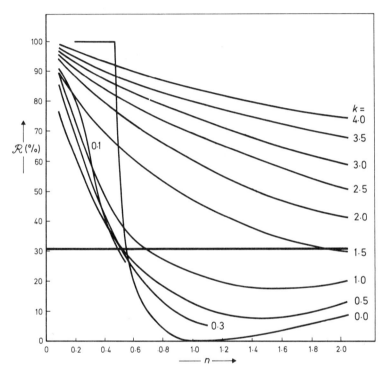

Fig. 48. $\mathscr{R}$ as a function of n at 20° angle of incidence (after W. R. Hunter, 1965).

radiation. He found that for a given n and k the sensitivity of the method is greatest using $\mathscr{R}_p$ and least using $\mathscr{R}_s$. Error studies showing the effects of nonparallelism and polarization of the incident radiation and error in reflectance measurement were made for $\mathscr{R}_p$ and $\mathscr{R}$, but not for $\mathscr{R}_s$ because the lack of sensitivity of the method for this component rendered it practically useless. It was found that the method is least sensitive to errors when using $\mathscr{R}_p$.

For measurements of the optical constants in the infra-red region a form of Kramers-Kronig dispersion analysis is generally used. The simplest form of the dispersion relation is

$$\theta(\omega_0) = \frac{\omega_0}{\pi} \int \frac{\log \mathscr{R}(\omega) - \log \mathscr{R}(\omega_0)}{\omega_0^2 - \omega^2} \, d\omega$$

where $\theta(\omega_0)$, the phase angle, relates the imaginary and real parts of the complex reflection amplitude.

$$r^*(\omega) = r(\omega)e^{i\theta(\omega)}, \; r(\omega) = \pm \sqrt{\mathscr{R}(\omega)}$$

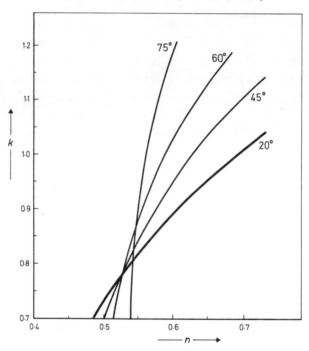

Fig. 49. Curves of constant reflectance for four angles of incidence (after W. R. Hunter, 1965).

at a given frequency ω_0. As these expressions indicate, θ depends on the reflectance amplitude $r(\omega)$ at all frequencies from zero to infinity and so it is not possible to measure it practically.

Approaches to this problem of defining frequency limits have been made by a number of workers. Robinson (1952), considering normally incident light, advocates measuring reflectance over a '... reasonably wide range of frequency', and using this data to calculate the phase angle at any frequency within the range.

The complex reflection coefficient r^* is then known in modulus and phase. Hence the complex refractive index

$$n^* = n - ik$$

may be completely determined through the reflection equation for normally incident light. Again graphs are necessary to derive the values of n and k, and Beattie and Conn (1955) have published families of such graphs.

The accuracy of the frequency-limiting method is rather poor and Gottlieb (1960) suggested a constant reflectance approximation for unobserved frequencies. Anderman *et al.* (1965), reviewing this method, admit an increase in accuracy and present their own extrapolation method for providing a 'wing correction'.

The Kramers-Kronig analysis considered so far has mainly been concerned with near-normal incidence radiation. This condition was chosen by workers, in preference to normal incidence, to avoid the use of beam splitters, particularly in the infra-red. However, the effect of the slight obliquity on the calculations has generally been ignored. That this is, in fact, reasonable has been shown by Berreman (1967). He describes a method of analysis for almost any angle of incidence (using polarized radiation) and illustrates his work by showing the relatively small error caused by neglecting a $15°$ angle of incidence.

For working in the ultra-violet (and the visible), Schmidt (1969) adopted the measurement of the maximum value of

$$\mathscr{R}_R = (\mathscr{R}_s - \mathscr{R}_p)/(\mathscr{R}_s + \mathscr{R}_p)$$

and the angle of incidence ϕ_B (Fig. 50). The method, using a rotating polarizer, was developed for use at room temperature to measure the optical constants of absorbing solids such as germanium (visible) and silicon (ultra-violet). Schmidt, commenting on the relative simplicity of his method, compared his results with those of Archer (1968)—determination of the ratio $\mathscr{R}_p/\mathscr{R}_s$ at different angles—and Potter (1964)—determination of the minimum $\mathscr{R}_p/\mathscr{R}_s$ and of the pseudo-Brewster angle. The comparison is shown in Fig. 51. The forms of the spectra are very similar and the 3–5 per cent difference in absolute values may be explained by the method of preparing the reflection specimens.

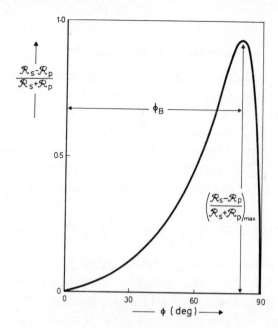

FIG. 50. Variation of $\mathscr{R}_R = (\mathscr{R}_s - \mathscr{R}_p)/(\mathscr{R}_s + \mathscr{R}_p)$ with the angle of incidence (after Schmidt, 1969).

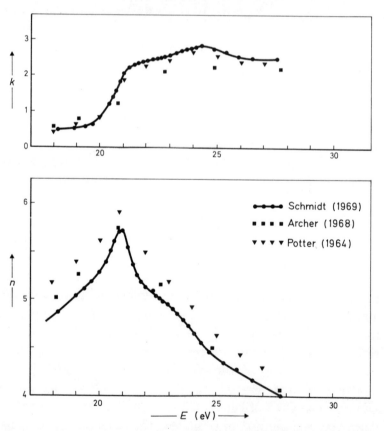

FIG. 51. The plot of optical constants n and k against energy E of germanium, measured at room temperature.

However, in the case of silicon serious disagreement with the values of the index of absorption measured by Dash and Newman (1955), using a transmission technique, were found. Schmidt suggested that although the form and absolute value of his *k*-spectrum were close to that determined byKramers-Kronig analysis, the discrepancy was due to his choice of reflectance function. That is, a small error in $\mathscr{R}_R$ causes a relatively large error in *k* in the region 0·54 micron. However, he concluded that the measurement of *n* was acceptably precise, because it is determined primarily by ϕ_B, and that, in general, the method gives results comparable with those obtained by using other, similar, methods (Archer, 1968 and Potter, 1964).

9.2. DETERMINATION OF SURFACE ROUGHNESS

In Part 1 we saw how no general theory of reflection could be derived for rough surfaces unless

1. They are very formalized structures, or
2. Statistical distributions of irregularities were assumed.

Several experimental investigations, with little theoretical basis, have been carried out on the relation between the roughness of machined metal surfaces, or ground glass surfaces, and the specular reflectance of these surfaces. These are described by Halling (1954), Hasunuma and Nara (1956), R. S. Hunter (1946), Guild (1940) and Middleton and Wyszecki (1957). Light in the visible was used and in most cases the reflectance was measured at oblique incidence, because at these wavelengths the surface irregularities are comparable in magnitude to the wavelength, and the amount of light that is specularly reflected at normal incidence is quite small. Under these circumstances the reflectance depends not only on the surface roughness but also on other aspects of the surface—for example the root mean square slope—so that measurements made have been only of limited usefulness as a method of determining surface roughness.

However, Bennett and Porteus (1961) suggested that if somewhat longer wavelengths are used for such surfaces, the characteristics of the surface other than roughness become unimportant and specular reflectance measurements at nearly normal incidence provide a simple and precise method of determining the root mean square roughness of a plane surface. The method is best applied to surfaces with a root mean square roughness of less than 125 μ. Bennett and Porteus give a theoretical basis for their work using the statistical treatment derived by Davies (1954).

'The surface is represented by a statistical model having the following properties:

1. The root mean square roughness σ, defined as the root mean square deviation of the surface from the mean surface level is small, compared with λ.

2. The surface is perfectly conducting and would have a specular reflectance of unity if it were smooth.

3. The distribution of heights of the surface irregularities is Gaussian about the mean.

4. The autocovariance function* of the irregularities is also Gaussian with standard deviation a.

The surface has the statistical properties of stationarity and ergodicity with respect to position along the surface.

'The expression for the specularly reflected component for a perfect conductor reduces, for the case of normal incidence, to $\exp(-(4\pi\sigma)^2/\lambda^2)$. Since no material is perfectly conducting, this is modified so that for an actual metal surface

$$\mathcal{R}_s = \mathcal{R}_0 \exp(-(4\pi\sigma)^2/\lambda^2) \qquad (9.1)$$

where $\mathcal{R}_s$ is the specular reflectance of the rough surface and $\mathcal{R}_0$ that of a perfectly smooth surface of the same material. The angular dependence of the diffusely reflected light can also be obtained. If $\mathcal{R}_0$ is included as before

$$r_D(\theta)\, d\theta = \mathcal{R}_0 2\pi^4 (a/\lambda)^2 (\sigma/\lambda)^2 (\cos\theta + 1)^4$$
$$\times \sin\theta \exp(-(\pi a \sin\theta)^2/\lambda^2)\, d\theta \qquad (9.2)$$

Here $r_D(\theta)$ refers to the fraction of the reflected light which is scattered into an angle between θ and $\theta + d\theta$ at an angle θ from the normal to the surface. If m is the root mean square slope of the profile of the surface the auto-covariance length a can be shown to be

$$a = \sqrt{2}\,\sigma/m \qquad (9.3)$$

---

*The autocovariance function is similar to his autocorrelation function but it is not normalized.

Therefore if the reflectance on the normal is measured with an instrumental acceptance angle $\Delta\theta$, for light at normal incidence, the contribution from diffuse reflectance is

$$\int_0^{\Delta\theta} r_D(\theta)\, d\theta = \mathscr{R}_0 2^5 \pi^4 (\sigma/\lambda)^4 (\Delta\theta)^2 / m^2 \tag{9.4}$$

Note that this contribution to the measured reflectance decreases very rapidly with increasing wavelength. For sufficiently long wavelengths the diffuse reflectance may therefore be neglected. The reflectance is then essentially specular and is given by equation (9.1). It depends only on σ and is not affected by the root mean square slope of the surface.

'Thus, in conclusion, the complete expression for the measured reflectance is

$$\mathscr{R} = \mathscr{R}_0 \exp(-(4\pi\sigma)^2/\lambda^2) + \mathscr{R}_0 2^5 \pi^4 (\sigma/\lambda)^4 (\Delta\theta)^2 / m^2 \tag{9.5}$$

'If reflectance measurements are made at sufficiently long wavelengths, σ can be calculated directly from the measured reflectance since equation (9.5) reduces to equation (9.1). At shorter wavelengths, however, the reflectance near the normal will be a function of both the surface roughness and the root mean square slope of the surface irregularities. By measuring the reflectance at two wavelengths, one of which is long enough for the effect of slope to be neglected, it should be possible to determine both the surface roughness and the root mean square slope of the surface irregularities.

'When the wavelength is long enough so that the diffuse reflectance may be neglected equation (9.5) may be written

$$\log_{10}(\mathscr{R}_0/\mathscr{R}) = \{(4\pi\sigma)^2/2{\cdot}303\}(1/\lambda^2) \tag{9.6}$$

Thus if $\mathscr{R}_0/\mathscr{R}$ is plotted on semi-log paper against $1/\lambda^2$, a straight line through the origin, with a slope that is directly proportional to σ^2, is obtained. It is convenient to use this equation to calculate the value of the root mean square roughness from the experimental values of the reflectance at normal incidence. Approximate values of the roughness may be obtained in this way even if the contribution from diffuse reflection is not negligible.'

In a later paper, Porteus (1963) extends the theory, with certain restrictions, to shorter wavelengths. It is shown that for many surfaces commonly encountered in practice the distribution of heights of surface irregularities can be satisfactorily determined from the specular reflectance at normal incidence.

9.3.   AUTOMOBILE SAFETY STANDARDS

In 1966 the United States General Services Administration issued its specifications for 'standard safety devices for automotive vehicles' (US Department of Commerce, 1966). A section of these specifications, devoted to the permissible reflectance values of fittings (horn ring, windscreen wiper arms, and so on) which were so positioned that they might reflect light into the driver's eyes, subsequently appeared as Federal Motor Vehicle Safety Standard FMVSS 107 (US Department of Commerce, 1967). Initial reaction to the imposition of this standard was to 'brush', or 'satinize', the offending bright metallic surfaces. This approach was based on the results of a number of investigations into the reflectance properties of this type of surface. Predictably, these tests, which, under the measurement conditions specified in the Standard, utilized a flat specimen with an ASTM 20° configuration (see § 8.7), found that satinized and other low-gloss finishes had a much reduced specular component of reflectance. Hence the glare effect was considerably diminished.

However, most automotive trim parts are not flat, and those which are (wiper arms) are of extremely small area. In the absence of a realistic test for this type of component, the use of satinized finishes was regarded as acceptable on the basis of the ASTM 20° condition.

However, techniques have now been developed for measuring the glare effect from both flat and curved surfaces—see Meldrum (1969). Using these techniques it is possible to investigate the true effectiveness of the finish treatment on production trim parts. For this purpose Meldrum compared three methods of measurement.

1.   *Glare Illumination*—A Pritchard photometer was used to measure the reflected light falling on a standard white target at a known distance from the surface under test. This method measures the amount of reflected light which reaches the driver's eyes from any given surface.

2. *Gloss*—The standard glossmeter method of measurement specified in FMVSS 107, which is a surface property measurement valid only for flat surfaces.

3. *Image Brightness*—A substitute gloss image method which converts measurements on curved surfaces to equivalent gloss units as specified for flat surfaces.

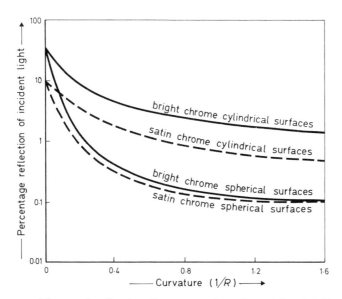

FIG. 52. Measured reflection from curved surfaces (after Meldrum, 1969).

Fig. 52 shows the results from method 1 and indicates that the percentage of incident light reflection from bright chrome spherical surfaces is similar to the percentage of incident light reflection from satin chrome spherical surfaces. This indicates further, that there is little or no benefit, in terms of glare reduction, when the finish on small-radius spherical surfaces is changed from bright chrome to satin chrome.

The reflection measurements from the cylindrical surfaces are larger than those from the spherical surfaces. Note, however, that as the cylindrical curvature (reciprocal of the radius measured in centimetres) increases beyond 0·4 cm^{-1}, there is a gradual reduction in incident light reflection and a fairly con-

sistent difference between the satin chrome and bright chrome
(Fig. 52).

Method 2 was implemented using a 20° Gardner glossmeter.
The satin chrome samples measured 22 units (FMVSS 107
allows 40 units with the 20° method of measurement). The two
flat bright chrome samples measured off-scale on the glossmeter.

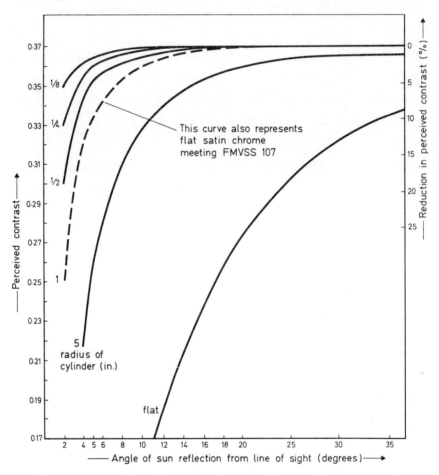

FIG. 53. Perceived contrast as affected by glare reflection from bright
chrome trim. Cylindrical shapes (after Duffy, 1969).

The results from method 3 showed consistency between the
measurements for flat and spherical surfaces for both types of
finish.

Both methods 2 and 3 measure surface properties and method 1
is the more relevant when considering the purpose of FMVSS

107. It shows that surface curvature (especially with small radii) has a greater effect on glare reduction than surface finish.

These findings are supported by the results of Saur and Dobrash (1969), who investigated the duration of afterimage disability following viewing of simulated sun reflections. They found that reductions in the glare effect produced by appropriate curvature of a bright surface were comparable to those produced by satinizing the surface.

Further evidence is given by the work of Duffy (1969), who used a computer to simulate the effect of sun reflections from chrome surfaces on visual performance in a variety of viewing situations. An example of his results is given in Fig. 53 for a bright chrome cylinder in a viewing situation appropriate to a sunny day. On the basis of his work Duffy has suggested that, rather than the existing Standard, the reflectivity standard for automotive trim should be expressed as a minimum level of visual performance, such as is measured by reduction in perceived contrast in a criterion viewing situation.

Working within the principles of the current Standard, however, it would appear that the choice of using surface finish or curvature as a means of reducing glare depends primarily on the feasible shape of the component. Bright cylindrical surfaces with less than 63·5 mm radius produce no more glare at the driver's eyes than flat satin chrome meeting the present Standard. Bright spherical surfaces reflect even less at the driver's eyes. Satinizing such surfaces provides no significant additional reduction of glare. Surfaces with, necessarily, less curvature, however, may still require some satin finish.

9.4. OPTICAL SYSTEM DESIGN

An optical system consists essentially of a number of surfaces representing interfaces between various combinations of air and glass materials. At each of these surfaces light may be lost through unwanted reflection. It is part of the optical designer's task to minimize this loss by applying the theory presented in earlier sections of this monograph. In effect, the problem reduces to the judicious choice of adjacent glasses, or the deposition of a calculated thin film, either case being a manipulation of the reflectance relation by means of varying the refractive index factors. The improvement possible with various designs of thin film is shown in Fig. 54 as a function of the number of elements in an optical system. The symbols HEA (High Efficiency Antireflection), V, and W, refer to proprietary designs of thin-film multilayers. The spectral performance of these thin films is illustrated in Fig. 55. From these figures it can be seen that the

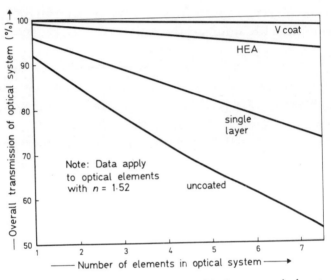

FIG. 54. Losses due to reflection in multi-element optical systems.

effect of using antireflection coatings can be a dramatic improvement in the brightness of the final image. A four-element optical system with coated surfaces will produce a 30 per cent brighter image than one without.

Going to the other extreme, mirrors may be incorporated in a system and loss from these elements is, of course, measured in terms of what they do not reflect. An example of the quality of mirror available at present is given in Fig. 56. Reflectances of this high order, maintained across a wide spectral band, find widespread use in modern optical systems. They can be employed as beam deflectors (in laser systems), return mirrors (for auto-collimation), and in fact any application where light beams must be manipulated without significant reduction in intensity or change in spectral content.

Between the extremes of elimination and optimization, the designer is often presented with the requirement for a specified reflectance performance. This could take a number of forms. An example was given earlier of a pair of interferometer mirrors designed to give 99 per cent reflectance at $22\frac{1}{2}°$ incidence using

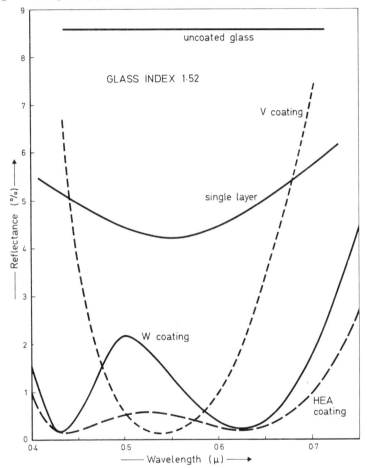

FIG. 55. Total reflection from two surfaces of a window coated with various antireflection film designs.

light of 0·4358 μ wavelength (Fig. 10). The same problem can be looked at in a slightly different way when designing a beam splitter with specific reflection properties. This type of optical element is used in systems where it is necessary to divide a single beam into two, each with the same spectral distribution as the parent beam. Fig. 57 shows a narrow-band beam splitter response.

A variant of the beam splitter is the colour separation filter used when it is desired to split the incident energy into two or more beams, each beam having a different spectral content or colour. Multilayer interference reflectors are well-suited for colour separation because all energy is either transmitted or reflected, with minimum absorption loss. The dichroic filter is so named because it divides the visible spectrum into two adjacent regions by reflecting one and transmitting the other (Fig. 58).

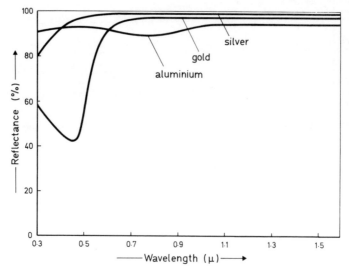

FIG. 56. The spectral response of metallic high reflectance mirrors.

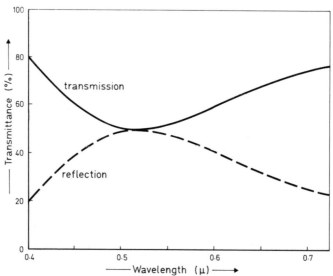

FIG. 57. The spectral response of a narrow-band beam splitter.

Trichroics are used to reflect a narrow wavelength band of energy while transmitting the energy at both longer and shorter wavelengths (Fig. 59). The separation of visible energy into its component parts has many military and industrial applications such as gunsight reflectors, signal separation in fire control systems, instrument display reflectors, map display systems, and colour printers.

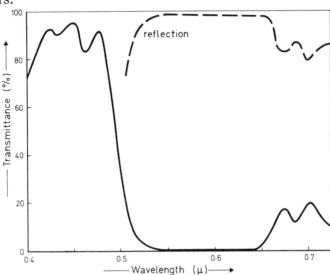

FIG. 58. The spectral response of a dichroic colour separation filter, reflecting the yellow region of the spectrum.

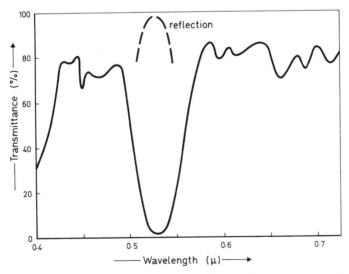

FIG. 59. The spectral response of a trichroic colour separation filter.

9.5. ILLUMINATING ENGINEERING

The task of illuminating engineers, or even architects and interior designers practising elements of the science, is to balance illumination sources and environment reflectance for the ultimate comfort of the human occupant. The word 'occupant' is used in the broadest sense since, very often, the engineer will be working out of doors, concerning himself with the adequacy of street and area lighting when taken in conjunction with the reflectances of materials constituting pavements, roads and other exterior surfaces.

Internally, reflection of light (even diffuse glare) from paper whilst reading, or from a poorly illuminated work surface, can be irritating and lead to eyestrain. The problem can be minimized by proper placement of the illuminating source and a knowledge of the reflectances of the surfaces within the field of view. This type of consideration is extremely relevant to the design of homes, schoolrooms, offices and factories, both in terms of the structure of the effective area, and the materials used within it.

9.6. REFLECTIONS ON THE ENVIRONMENT

It may appear to be a truism that non-luminous objects are only seen by virtue of the light they reflect. An appreciation of this fact, however, opens up a considerable field for the measurement and application of reflectance data relating to the visibility of objects in a natural environment.

This aspect of reflectance measurement has been pursued, both in Britain and the United States, as an aid to the detection and recognition of military targets in natural surroundings. Assuming that the illumination characteristics of the sky are known (a not inconsiderable assumption), then a knowledge of terrain reflectance, both specular and diffuse, and the reflectances of typical military targets, enables the calculation of inherent target contrast. This may then be directly related to the probability of detecting and recognizing the targets. Unfortunately, or fortunately (depending on your role as attacker or defender), the person searching for a target would normally be presented with a considerable variety of terrain in any particular scene. Thus any

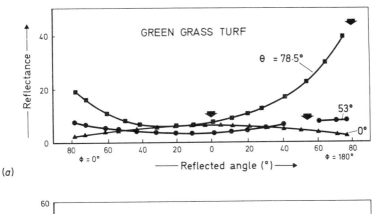

(a)

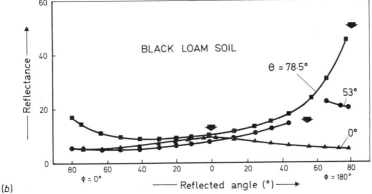

(b)

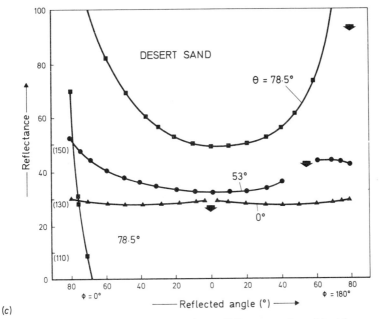

(c)

Fig. 60. Directional reflectance at three different angles of incidence (principal plane, wavelength 0·6430 μ). $\phi = 0°$ ... Forward scatter $\phi = 180°$ ... Back scatter. (From Coulson, 1966.)

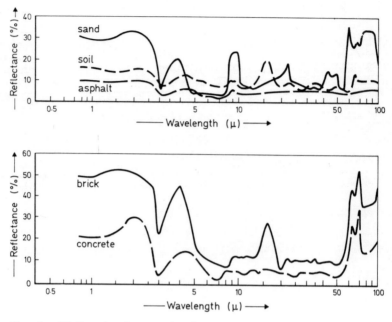

FIG. 61. Bi-directional spectral reflectance coefficients for a variety of surfaces (from Bartman, 1967).

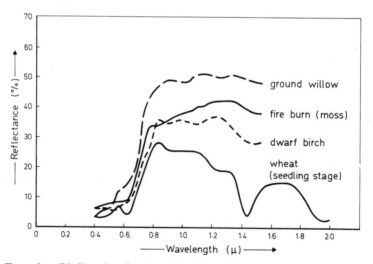

FIG. 62. Bi-directional spectral reflectance curves for vegetation (from Bartman, 1967).

model of the scene would have to incorporate reflectance data on all types of likely to occur natural surfaces. Some examples of this type of data are given in Table 2 and Figs. 60–62. The table was compiled from the results of a number of workers including Krinov (1953), Coulson *et al.* (1965), Coulson (1966), Gordon *et al.* (1966), and Bartman (1967). Instruments used for these various measurements included the telephotometer, for *in situ* work, and the goniophotometer for selected samples in the more controlled conditions of a laboratory.

There are, of course, situations when the desire to hide something, to lose it in its natural surroundings, arises from innocent, indeed laudable, motives. It is an unfortunate fact that gasometers, factories, electricity substations, and other essential elements of our developed society must occasionally be located in areas of beautiful countryside. It would be interesting to consider an application of the techniques outlined above to ascribe an obtrusiveness factor to a building in relation to its surroundings. If this were done in the planning stage then the magnitude of the factor could provide ammunition for the conservationist who would relate it to an acceptable standard of obtrusiveness. In any event the application of these techniques should point the way to minimizing the visual effect of buildings which would otherwise be an eyesore.

TABLE 2. Summary of Reflectance Data for Earth Surface Features

Surface	Bi-directional Reflectance	Spectral Characteristics	Total Reflectance
Soils, sand, etc.	1. Back and forward scattering 2. Sand has larger forward scattering 3. Loam has small forward scattering 4. Moisture increases forward and reduces backscattering	1. Increasing to $1\ \mu$ 2. Decreasing above $2\ \mu$	1. 5–45 per cent 2. Moisture decreases reflectance by 5–20 per cent 3. Smoother surfaces have higher reflectance
Vegetation	1. Back scattering 2. Small forward scattering	1. Small below $0\cdot5\ \mu$ 2. Peak at $0\cdot5$–$0\cdot55\ \mu$ 3. Chlorophyll absorption at $0\cdot68\ \mu$ 4. Sharp increase at $0\cdot7\ \mu$ 5. Decrease above $2\ \mu$ 6. Variation with growing season	1. 5–25 per cent 2. Diurnal effects, maximum reflectance at large angles 3. Marked annual variation
Water	1. Back and forward scattering large at large angles	1. Maximum at $0\cdot5$–$0\cdot7\ \mu$ 2. Dependent on turbidity	1. Small reflectance 2. Maximum at high angles 3. Dependent on turbidity
Snow and ice	1. Diffuse component plus specular component 2. Specular component increases with incidence angle	1. Decreases slightly with increasing wavelength 2. Large variability depending on purity, wetness and physical condition	1. Variable, 25–100 per cent

Bibliography

ANDERMAN, G., CARON, A., and DOWS, D. A., 1965, *J. Opt. Soc. Am.*, **55**, 1210.

ARCHER, R. J., 1968, *Manual of Ellipsometry* (Gaertner Scientific Corporation, Chicago).

ASTM (American Society for Testing Materials), 1966, *Book of Standards*, Part 21.

BARKMAN, E. F., 1959, Reynolds Metals Company, Metallurgical Research Report 571–13A.

BARTMAN, F. L., 1967, *The Reflectance and Scattering of Solar Radiation by the Earth.* (University of Michigan, Tech. Report 058-63-11-T).

BEATTIE, J. R., and CONN, G. K. T., 1955, *Phil. Mag.*, **44**, 222.

BECKMANN, P., and SPIZZICHINO, A., 1963, *The Scattering of Electromagnetic Waves from Rough Surfaces* (Pergamon Press Inc., New York).

BENNETT, H. E., and KOEHLER, W. F., 1960, *J. Opt. Soc. Am.*, **50**, 1.

BENNETT, H. E., and PORTEUS, J. O., 1961, *J. Opt. Soc. Am.*, **51**, 123.,

BERTHOLD, J., 1969, *App. Optics*, **8**, 1919.

BERREMAN, D. W., 1967, *App. Optics*, **6**, 1519.

BLACKWELL, H. R., 1967, *App. Optics*, **6**, 1443.

BORN, M., and WOLF, E., 1964, *Principles of Optics* (Pergamon, London).

BOUGUER, P., 1961, *The Gradation of Light* (University of Toronto Press). Translation.

BRIDGEMAN, A., 1961, *Die Farbe*, **10**, 243.

BRODERSEN, S., 1953, *J. Opt. Soc. Am.*, **43**, 877.

BRODERSEN, S., 1954, *J. Opt., Soc. Am.*, **44**, 22.

CHINMAYANANDAM, T. K., 1919, *Phys. Rev.*, **13**, 96

CHRISTIE, J. S., 1969, *App. Optics*, **8**, 1777.

CHWOLSON, O. D., 1922, *Lehrb. d. Physik*, Bd II, 2, (2 Aufl.), 716 (Vieweg, Braunschweig).

CONN, G. K. T., and EATON, G. K., 1954, *J. Opt. Soc. Am.*, **44**, 484.

COULSON, K. L., 1966, *App. Optics*, **5**, 905.

COULSON, K. L. *et al.*, 1965, *J. Geophys. Res.*, **70**, 4601.

CRAWFORD, B. H., and MARSH, J. L., 1957, *N.P.L. Report, Op. Met.* 2.

DASH, W. C., and NEWMAN, R., 1955, *Phys. Rev.*, **99**, 1151.

DAVIES, H., 1954, *Proc. Inst. Elec. Engrs.*, **101**, 209.

DUFFY, W., 1969, *App. Optics*, **8**, 1803.

EBERHARDT, W. H., 1950, *J. Opt. Soc. Am.*, **40**, 172.

GIER, J. T., DUNKLE, R. V., and BEVANS, J. T., 1954, *J. Opt. Soc. Am.*, **44**, 558.

GORDON, J. I. *et al.*, 1966, *App. Optics*, **5**, 919.

GOTTLIEB, M., 1960, *J. Opt. Soc. Am.*, **50**, 343.

GUILD, J., 1940, *J. Sci. Instr.*, **17**, 178.

HALLING, J., 1954, *J. Sci. Instr.*, **31**, 318.

HAMMER, K., 1943, *Z. Tech. Phys.*, **24**, 169.

HARDY, A. C., and YOUNG, F. M., 1949, *J. Opt. Soc. Am.*, **39**, 265.

HARRISON, V. G. W., 1945, *Definition and Measurement of Gloss* (PATRA, Cambridge).

HARTMAN, P. L., and LOGOTHETIS, E., 1964. *App. Optics*, **3**, 255.

HASS, G., JACOBUS, G. F., and HUNTER, W. R., 1967, *J. Opt. Soc. Am.*, **57**, 758.

HASUNUMA, H., and NARA, J., 1956, *J. Phys. Soc. Japan*, **11**, 69.

HULBURT, E. O., 1934, *J. Opt. Soc. Am.*, **24**, 35.

HUMPHREYS-OWEN, S. P. F., 1961, *Proc. Phys. Soc.*, **77**, 949.

HUNTER, R. S., 1940, *J. Opt. Soc. Am.*, **30**, 536.

HUNTER, R. S., 1946, *J. Opt. Soc. Am.*, **36**, 178.

HUNTER, W. R., 1965, *J. Opt. Soc. Am.*, **55**, 1197.

HUNTER, W. R., 1967, *App. Optics*, **6**, 2140.

INGERSOLL, L. R., 1921, *J. Opt. Soc. Am.*, **5**, 213.

JOHNSON, F. S., WATANEBE, K., and TOUSEY, R., 1951, *J. Opt. Soc. Am.*, **41**, 702.

JUDD, D. B., 1967, *J. Opt. Soc. Am.*, **57**, 445.

KRINOV, E. L., 1953, Tech. Transl. TT 439. National Research Council of Canada, Ottawa.

LONGUET-HIGGINS, M. S., 1960a, *J. Opt. Soc. Am.*, **50**, 838.

LONGUET-HIGGINS, M. S., 1960b, *J. Opt. Soc. Am.*, **50**, 845.

MELDRUM, J. F., 1969, *App. Optics*, **8**, 1791.

MESSNER, R., 1943, *Zeiss Nachr.*, **4** (H9), 253.

MIDDLETON, W. E. K., and WYSZECKI, G., 1957, *J. Opt. Soc. Am.*, **47**, 1020.

MOON, P., and SPENCER, D. E., 1945a, *J. Opt. Soc. Am.*, **35**, 399.

MOON, P., and SPENCER, D. E., 1945b, *J. Opt. Soc. Am.*, **35**, 597.

OLDHAM, M. S., 1951, *J. Opt. Soc. Am.*, **41**, 673.

PORTEUS, J. O., 1963, *J. Opt. Soc. Am.*, **53**, 1394.

POTTER, R. F., 1964, *J. Opt. Soc. Am.*, **54**, 904.

PRESTON, J. S., 1936, *J. Sci. Instr.*, **13**, 368.

PRITCHARD, B. S., 1955, *J. Opt. Soc. Am.*, **45**, 356.

PURCELL, J. D., 1953, *J. Opt. Soc.*, *Am.*, **43**, 1166.

REID, C. D., and MCALISTER, E. D., 1959, *J. Opt. Soc. Am.*, **49**, 78.

RENNILSON, J. J., HOLT, H. E., and MORRIS, E. C., 1968, *J. Opt. Soc. Am.*, **58**, 747.

ROBINSON, T. S., 1952, *Proc. Phys. Soc.*, **68**, 910.

RODRIGUEZ, A. R., PARMELEE, C. W., and BADGER, A. E., 1943, *J. Am. Ceram. Soc.*, **26**, 137.

SAUR, R. L., and DOBRASH, S. M., 1969, *App. Optics*, **8**, 1799.

SCHMIDT, E., 1969, *App. Optics*, **8**, 1905.

SCHRECKENDGUST, J. G., and GOWING, D. M., 1958, *J. Opt. Soc. Am.*, **48**, 241.

SCHUSTER, A., 1905, *Astrophys. J.*, **21**, 197.

SHAW, J. E., and BLEVIN, W. R., 1964, *J. Opt. Soc. Am.*, **54**, 334.

SHOULEJKIN, W., 1924, *Phil. Mag.*, 6th series, **48**, 307.

SMITH, A., 1960, *J. Opt. Soc. Am.*, **50**, 862.

SPENCER, D. E., and GRAY, S. M., 1960, *Illum. Engineering*, April 1960.

STRONG J., 1938, *Procedures in Experimental Physics* (Prentice-Hall).

SWINDELL, P., 1968, *App. Optics*, **7**, 943.

TINGLE, W. H., and GEORGE, D. J., 1965, S.A.E. Report 650513.

TINGLE, W. H., and POTTER, F. R., 1961, *Prod. Eng.*, March 1961.

Todd, E. P., 1959, *J. Opt. Soc. Am.*, **49**, 491.

Tousey, R., 1957, *J. Opt. Soc. Am.*, **47**, 261.

U.S. Department of Commerce, 1966, *Federal Register*, **31**, number 136.

U.S. Department of Commerce, 1967, *Federal Register*, **32**, number 23.

Walsh, J. W. T., 1958, *Photometry* (Constable and Co. Ltd, London).

Weeks, R. F., 1958, *J. Opt. Soc. Am.*, **48**, 775.

Weinstein, W. T., 1954, *Vacuum*, **4**, 3.

Wright, H. R., 1900, *Phil. Mag.*, **49**, 199.

Wright, W. D., 1954, *Opt. Acta*, **1**, 102.

Zipin, R. B., 1966, *App. Optics*, **5**, 1954.

Index